UNFOLDMENT OF THE
GREAT WITHIN

Experienced Thinking for Your
Self Development

by
Bernard Jensen, Ph.D.

D1452861

PUBLISHED BY:

Bernard Jensen, Ph.D.
24360 Old Wagon Road
Escondido, CA 92027 USA

First Edition

BERNARD JENSEN, Publisher
24360 Old Wagon Road
Escondido, CA 92027 USA

ISBN 0-932615-24-4

I would like to dedicate this book
to my mentor and teacher, Dr. V. G. Rocine,
who has given me enlarged mental faculties through my
following him. He has made me feel, within myself, that I
can go within and come out a greater person. It is here that
all great things come through us. He taught me that God
can only do for you what He can do through you.

We must develop the Great Within so the great things may
happen in your life.

—Dr. Bernard Jensen

Introduction by Napoleon Hill

Author of Think and Grow Rich and the Master Key to Riches

There seldom appears a book which one can recommend so wholeheartedly and unreservedly as this one-in-a-million book, Unfoldment of the Great Within, by Dr. Bernard Jensen.

In recommending this lifestyle of living is almost as though I were praising my own work, as the success principles embodied are fundamentally identical with my own. As we all know, success cannot be really sound without consideration of the physical, mental and spiritual aspects. One without the others is a hollow success. You cannot reach the peak of attainment with a sick body regardless of mind brilliancy. Likewise a healthy body without a well-trained mind also has its limitations.

Yet this book must not be construed as simply a success book. It teaches sane how-to-live principles which inevitably lead to successful living. These sound principles truly make living the joy it should be. Humanity would profit if this book were on every bookshelf and in every library.

So it is with a feeling of public spiritedness that I introduce to you Unfoldment of the Great Within and its brilliant author, Dr. Bernard Jensen—assured in my heart that yours will be a healthier and happier life for having become acquainted with them both.

❖

FOREWORD

I feel it is a special privilege for me to publish *Unfoldment of the Great Within*, presenting some of the teachings of Dr. V. G. Rocine, my greatest teacher, together with my own thoughts and philosophy.

I owe much of my success in the healing art, my understanding of people and my philosophy of life to Rocine. Homeopath, author, lecturer and teacher, Rocine was my teacher, mentor and friend through the decades of the 30s and 40s, and out of all his students, he told me I was one of his best. This has meant more to me than a Nobel prize.

Rocine stood out from "the crowd," and this book shows how he did it. If you study it diligently, this book will change your life, as it did mine.

Before immigrating from his native Norway to the United States, Rocine studied in European universities to gather from the best minds of his time the most up-to-date research and ideas concerning the influences that make man what he is. He looked into chemical topology, food chemistry, anatomy and physiology, brain functions, religion, philosophy, social studies and who knows what else, adding his own observations and experiences to what he learned in the classroom. Rocine knew more about people than anyone I ever met.

Rocine knew how foods and the chemicals in them affected the temperaments people displayed. I have often heard him talk about the kinds of behaviors and behavioral changes that are shaped by diet, climate, altitude, weather, work and other such factors. He was a keen observer, a master of grasping and interpreting how the spiritual, mental and physical faculties were being affected from the outside or inside. He could almost predict what strengths and weaknesses a person had from looking at him or her.

If I were to summarize all I have learned concerning the great needs of mankind in my 84 years on this Earth, this is

1

what I would say: We owe humanity every effort, every little push we can give it, to bring it to the highest level of existence. We find this has to begin from within. If we could only realize it is within ourselves that we learn to carry other people and become our brother's keeper, we would also realize we must go within to find a means of guiding others to a higher path. Only in this way will our world become a better place to live. It all starts in our personal world, the world within. This is where war or peace is first declared. This is where we will choose which one to bring out and develop.

Before there can be peace on Earth, it has to begin within. Can you see this?

The most important thing I can tell you is that all we can offer the world must come from an unfoldment of the *Great Within*. Here is where the real training comes from. Here is where we're going to make a better world. Here is where we're going to make a better body. Here is where we are going to be reaching for the better things in life, and this little book is one of the finest things I have written to help you get started. If you were going to recommend a special book to someone to help get them started on the higher road to health, harmony and happiness, this would be your best choice. It is within that we go with all our failures, faults and frailties and learn to turn them into stepping stones to a higher and better life. We can't expect to get all our good from the outside. This little book teaches you how to go within and, starting with your innermost self, grow from within out.

One of the greatest axioms of life is that we live on what we pour out. If you only pour out negative, distrustful and destructive thoughts, that is what you will attract. But if you pour out positive and uplifting thoughts and ideas, you will attract the higher things in life. If you want the finer and higher things in life, this book will tell you how to take a few upward steps each day of your life. This is very important.

If I was going to take a person to be my patient, I would like to have one who understood the principles brought out in this book. It is from these principles of the deeper life within that we make the changes that bring healing by seeking the best for ourselves.

You must learn to believe that you deserve the best. When you believe you deserve the best, I can teach you how to get well and stay well. You must prepare to move, to grow, to get out of the past. You have to move into a higher consciousness. This, I believe, is where I can help you most. You cannot help but have a better life after you have read this book.

When we learn to bring in ease of mind, then we begin to push disease out of our bodies. We should know how to start a new life and new day, and nothing would give me greater pleasure than to see you become a wiser, healthier and better person.

It is my wish and prayer that each day you may become a better person, learning to enjoy more of the better things in life. Noble thoughts take time to develop, but we must start somewhere, and this is the best day to begin the rest of your life. I'm positive that I'm going to be a blessing to you through this book, and you will have the pleasure of discovering and recognizing each blessing for yourself.

It is through my writings that I have been able to reach and help so many thousands of people by teaching them how to help themselves. And for those aspiring to learn to lift others, this book can be a lamp to light your path. I believe the destiny of your life is to have everything good coming to you. I'm convinced that we are measured by our endeavors, so let us set our minds and hearts on the higher things, and even greater things will come. This is the heritage of every true seeker.

CONTENTS

LESSON 12

LESSON 13

LESSON 14

INTRODUCTION

THE UNFOLDMENT OF THE GREAT WITHIN

It is a rare individual these days who understands that all good, all authority and all prosperity ultimately come from a spiritual source. In his time, V. G. Rocine was one of those rare individuals, and this book's purpose is to teach us how to get back to that spiritual source and recover the dignity and the nobility that make up every person's true spiritual heritage.

So many people find they are not accomplishing in life the goals and plans they set out to fulfill in their younger days. They may be called misfits in life. They live from year to year, finding they are a square peg trying to fit in a round hole. It has never been the intention of the Most High for life to be a tragedy. But, sometimes we are slow in learning our lessons.

Spiritual lessons are sometimes only valuable to those who have tried everything they know and failed. Sometimes we have to come to the end of our hopes to realize we need help from the Most High. "Man's extremity is God's opportunity," they say.

But, where can they go for help?

It is written, "The Kingdom of God is within you."

What does this mean? We find out that Rocine is following this way of thinking when he says, "We must go to the Great Within."

That is, we seek the Most High in the Great Within, where his Kingdom may be found.

It may come as a surprise to you that the "Unfoldment of the Great Within" begins—in Lesson 1—with instruction on brain building and self training. Rocine felt that the brain was the physical structure the Great Within through which the Kingdom of God operates. So, we see that the mind, set apart for service to the Most High, needs a physical vehicle to operate through. That is, God can only do for you what he can do through you.

In other words, "Unfoldment of the Great Within," that process of self exaltation which lifts a person into harmony with the Most High, is assisted by taking proper care of the brain, whose faculties or centers are important in the growth and change of the individual and even in the level of a person's consciousness.

The goal here is nothing less than the full realization of the highest potential in man, of whom it is written that he was created in the likeness of the Most High.

Rocine views the ennoblement of man as a process involving not only the spiritual side of man but also the physical. Can we bring forth the full potential of a person who lacks adequate circulation of blood to the brain areas? A lack of nutrients to feed the brain? An everyday diet incapable of meeting the brain's basic needs for its specialized tissues to be fed? Rocine says, "no," because man is a unified whole, including body, mind and spirit.

This is at no time more obvious than when a person is experiencing severe depression and has reached the "poor me" state of self pity. Is it only the mind that is affected? Look at the posture of such a person. Notice how they stand and walk. Recall the expression of the face. The appetite disappears, the eyes grow dull, sickness becomes more frequent. There is no talk of spiritual values or prayer in the normal course of such dejection. Instead, what has begun in the mind has influenced the body and spirit as well.

We must take care of body, mind and spirit when a disturbance occurs at any level. Before we think or smile something must move in the brain, and we find that the brain is the control center for the rest of the body. We must recognize this.

WE ENTER IN AND WE COME FORTH

"Nothing succeeds like success," they say, and it is a great thing to realize that within us may lie latent powers. Our body is like a tabernacle, and the most high dwells in it.

To be awakened to the solutions of our problems and to be uplifted by the Almighty, we must enter into his dwelling place. We enter into the Great Within, seeking the touch of the Most High. Then we come forth, a different person, a better person.

Many times people go through life never realizing their divine potential, the wonderful inheritance available to all.

The greatness of the teaching in this book is that you begin from where you are in life and you learn to become the person you are destined to be by the unfoldment of the Great Within. We enter in and we come forth, and we recognize that coming into the light is what we pray for, reach out for and come forth into.

LESSON 1

BRAIN BUILDING AND SELF TRAINING—
AN IMPERATIVE DUTY

Cell building in the brain requires:

1. A special kind of mind exercise.
2. A liberal flow of blood to the brain.
3. A brain building diet.
4. Application at regular hours.

Mitosis is cell building, also called cell segmentation. This is nature's process of building a man of a little baby. Cytologists inform us that a baby weighing about ten pounds is a little bundle of cells reaching the incredible number of from three to four billion cells, all made during the period of pregnancy (in two hundred and eighty days). Here we can see that on an average, nature builds about fourteen and one-half million cells each twenty-four hours in the unborn, when the cell "factory" works day and night without cessation. Nature knows no rest, no vacation.

Again, cell scientists, including Mr. Richardson, a great cell authority, informs us that the cells in a fully-developed brain number approximately twelve-thousand million cells. As the brain divides itself into forty-five compartments, or faculty centers, we can determine from this information that each faculty center has about two-hundred-and-sixty-seven million brain cells for its functionality. If a brain center has only about one-hundred million brain cells at its command, the brain power is below par to the extent of about one-hundred-and-sixty-seven million brain cells. Imagine that most of the brain cells in one faculty are asleep. How would that man feel, act, talk and think? But suppose we can arouse his sleeping brain cells and build in new cells by the millions by: (1) special thought exercises; (2) by charging his brain with good blood; (3) by giving him a special brain-building diet; (4) and, by diligent application.

Is it not natural that we would:
Unfold his genius?
Lead him to higher heights?
Illuminate his *Great Within*?
Ennoble his character?
Develop self confidence?
Overcome his bashfulness and timidity?
Train his nerves?
Quicken the senses?
Enlarge his views?
Heighten aspirations?

Is it not natural that we would:
Increase his talent?
Exalt the soul?
Ennoble his personality?
Make him more popular and influential?
Increase his wealth?
Double and triple his efficiency?
Bring him fame and fortune?
Increase his business?
Qualify him for important positions?

We, or really he, would do it all by processes of cell building. He would soon unfold his *Great Within* and reconstruct himself!

The chemist tells us that we live as we die, and when we stop dying, we stop living, that we melt away like candles, and are constantly being rebuilt.

IS DEVELOPMENT POSSIBLE?

Some men believe that the brain cannot be developed. The chemist informs us that the life of a brain cell, or any cell, is only six weeks. How then, does it happen that our brain "box" is not empty long before the age of ten? Or why does the blacksmith's arm become stronger by constant use of the hammer? Does not a bone fracture conglutinate, a wound heal, a scab, a sore, an ulcer, a cut, or a scratch heal, close up and consolidate by methods of mitosis and the flow of good blood to the injured parts? Can the pugilist develop his muscles? Can lungs be developed? Does a baby grow into a man? Does the blood flow to the brain the same as it does to the bones or to the muscles? The blood flows to any part of the body or brain that is being exercised. Are we right? If not, why do you recommend physical culture for men and calisthenics for women? Or why do we eat? Is not the brain washed with fresh blood daily, the same as the muscles? Muscular movements draw blood to the muscles and develop them. Are we right? Thought exercises draw blood to the brain and develop it. Why not? Thoughts have their roots in the blood. Genius is fed by the blood and by a normal brain diet. Are we correct? A special kind of thought exercises develop a special brain center. Why not?

BRAIN BUILDING THE HOPE OF THE LOWLY

Brain building is the hope of the unfortunate, of the man of failure. It enables us to earn more, live longer, climb higher, accomplish more and die a nobler death. It revolutionizes our life. Indeed, each man owes himself *some system of culture,* to arouse his sleeping forces and latent brain cells, or his energies will be wasted, brain cells will shrink and die, his joints will become rusty and he will become the victim of failure. Genius cannot be purchased, brain cannot be bought, health is not stored up in bottles on a drugstore shelves, nor is there any brain food in doughnuts, coffee, cake, rheumatic meat and white bread. Neither can we unfold the *Great Within* or develop personality by attending cinemas, dances, shows and sensational dramas, though such sports may be pleasing to the carnal man. Nor can we depend upon nature, or people to do anything for us. No one can eat for us, circulate our blood, digest our food, breathe for us, sleep for us or study for us. We must do it *ourselves,* or it will not be done.

COME OUT FROM THE GREAT WITHIN

It is a great thing to realize that within us may lie latent powers. We have reached a point of satisfaction knowing we have been traveling a lifelong path of achievement. I have often thought we are measured by our endeavors, being taught there are great things within us, if only they could be expressed. Our body is a tabernacle and it is the Great Spirit that dwells within.

We realize the physical body is so important to take care of, yet we become discouraged and disgruntled. We live in despair on a lower-life level. We are told often to "come ye out," demonstrate a different *inner self,* recognize your *self.* There is something *great within* you that should be expressed.

Through my lifelong studies, I have come to recognize the greatest curiosity to be is that we live on what we pour out. But, if we are pouring out hate, fear or disturbance, a panic is sending the body into turmoil and revolution. A disturbance within causes more trouble in the person that expresses it than the person that receives it. Every cell feels what we pour out.

It is time to go within. This is one of the greatest axioms I have ever come upon and endeavored to develop. Start from within and "come ye out."

We certainly do not feel good when we are living in a poor within. When we feel good within we feel rich. It is one of the greatest riches in life. When we attach ourselves to something such as serving others, uplifting them, caring for them and just plain doing good, we are surrounding ourselves with riches. It is very necessary that we recognize another more fruitful environment within us.

It might be said that we are keeping up with the Jones'. Living in this society, we are following what we have been taught, we live in rags and impoverishment. We hear the old saying, "there goes a poor soul," and think there goes a person low in spirit.

As we go on in life, we do not question or investigate the world within, in and of itself. We only function on the surface without going deep within. We do not go into the Secret Place of the Most High. We do not take to our *Great Within* and come out changed with spirit aglow, spreading good cheer and transforming others as well.

We should come out feeling good that we have accomplished something and feeling that we are somebody. We can even be proud of ourself and say that this is a beautiful being within me. I have learned this to be true from a spiritual standpoint; and, yes, from a physical and mental standpoint as well. I recognize, from a spiritual standpoint, it is the Father within me that doeth the work, as our great Master has taught us. It is a matter of going within and coming out to spread the Master's work.

Isn't it possible that we could be a better person tomorrow than we are today? Where are the pearls of great price? Where does wisdom really exist? Where is that wisdom that comes from the wise domain? Our wise home? It is in the secret place of the Most High, it is here that we become exalted. It is here that we go to the high road in life. It is here that we get our directions deciding whether it should be the high road or the low road. It is here that we make our decisions.

We must come to the conclusion that we have developed the inner self so we have something to depend on and that it is "I." When I see myself in the mirror, it is not a shell, it is the image from within. The size of our nose, shape of the ears, height of our eyebrows, length of our legs or the shape of our bodies, defines only the shell. Yes, the shell must be well cared for and nurtured.

All of my life I have taught people how to build a new body, new cell structure and rebuild old tissue, to take on a quality healing for replacing the old for the new. Now we gain control over our life through the mental and spiritual aspects working within our bodies. No one really feels good when hating others. We would all feel better if we could have a forgiving attitude, blessing others.

Our mind is the headquarters. Of all our getting, we must get into the mind. The mind is going to lead us into trouble or into upliftment. It can lead us out of trouble and give us the spiritual growth to feel happy and satisfied. We will feel good in achievement and knowledge, and find peace. We can only find that pleasure by seeking the *Great Within* that exists deep inside. It is here that we must have the elevation to develop into exaltation. It is here that we must seek the higher road and reach to the higher power. The acknowledgement and use of this elevated thinking will bring a greater understanding needed with our family, our jobs and associations with other people. This is the greater work meant for us to do when we were placed on this Earth. It is here that we unfold our talents, achieve ability, become leaders and lead ourselves to a better life.

Our endeavors are going to be distinctly successful when developed from this *Great Within*. It is here that we start onward and upward. We will be measured by the influence we have in this world and in our family. Teaching others by knowledge means very little when compared to how we can influence others by our example.

Once we learn to be congenial, and do this in our own silence and quiet of our mind, reaching within, we will see our own genius unfold. We will go forward to higher heights, reaching for that which is approved by God. We can even bring fame and fortune to ourselves. We can build and ennoble our personality. We can overcome shyness.

This new development is possible only through the development of the *Great Within*, reaching for the very best in you. You must apply yourself, recognizing that through self exaltation you will grow out of the past and into the new. I am sure that many people would like to come into a new life. This particular course is going to be the greatest thing we have ever thought could come to us, leading us out of the problems and troubles we may be experiencing. It may bring us from the place of inner poverty we've been living in, to the secret place where there is vigor, life and beauty, harmony flowing over the entire body through the mind, and spirit. Our body is a servant to the mind and to the spirit. We can be ready for a new day with a renewed mind, seeking higher values and becoming more of a noble man.

Confucius taught us to seek the higher values in life as did so many of our wonderful teachers in the past.

Dr. V. G. Rocine, my greatest teacher, gave me these thoughts in the beginning, concerning the ennobling of the mind. It was he who showed me I could change my mind and come into the light to see greater things from a health, harmony and happiness standpoint. It was not just for me that these lessons were taught. It was for all of mankind.

While visiting India we were told, by one of the great master teachers, contentment within is the one great element we should seek. I know that each and every one of us would like to have inner peace. Our Greatest Master teaches us to "come ye out," serve others, so the deaf hear and the blind see. This can only be done when we have elevated and exalted ourselves to a higher level giving others faith and confidence. This must start within ourself.

I hope and pray this course will touch you in a way that will bring you close to the Great One who is willing to give you this power and energy, and who will always be with you.

I want you to have the very best. There is no reason why you shouldn't be successful, physically, mentally and spiritually. It is to this path we now set out in a direction that will lead to the *Great Within*.

Abou Ben Adhem

Abou Ben Adhem, (may his tribe increase!)
Awoke one night from a deep dream of peace
And saw within the moonlight in his room
Making it rich and like a lily in bloom
An angel, writing a book of gold;
Exceeding peace had made Ben Adhem bold,
And to the presence in the room he said,
"What writest thou?" — The vision raised its head,
And with a look made of all sweet accord,
Answered, "The names of those who love the Lord."
"And is mine one?" said Abou. "Nay, not so,"
Replied the angel. Abou spoke more low,
But cheerily still and said, "I pray thee, then,
Write me as one who loves his fellow men."
The angel wrote and vanished. The next night
It came again with a great wakening light.
And showed the names of those whom love of God had blessed,
and lo! Ben Adhem's name led all the rest!

Much of this course has been taken from Dr. Rocine's notes. I am ever grateful for his recognition of me as one of his finest students. It is a great honor for me to be able to carry on with his work and to give to others so much that he has given to me.

Nature does nothing for man except supply him with earth, air, water, food, light, sunshine and some kind of habitation, as for instance, a cave. Man must till his own soil, raise his own grain, fruit and vegetables, build his own home, frame his own shanty, or live like a wild beast.

Nature does nothing for gardens. She permits anything to grow, especially bugs, germs and weeds. Were it not for the diligent and vigilant gardener and his hoe, plant diseases and bugs would soon kill the tender plants in field and garden. If we forget our teeth they decay. If we leave the fruit standing, it rots, if we live on "bub and grub," we soon go to the medical purgatory, or to the cold grave or both. Doctors cannot cure us; pills cannot save us; technique cannot reconstruct us.

Leave the costly automobile in the sun, heat, rain, snow, frost, wind, and what will be its value in a short time? Let your promising son run wild on the streets while the progressive mother attends card tables and political meetings and soon thistles grow in his brain and he runs up against some policeman's club, or perhaps to die in the gas chamber. Leave bread standing and it molds. *Do nothing for yourself and you will soon be a mere shadow of your former self.* Forget the lungs, air, altitude and a lung-building diet and soon germs consume the lungs, and you are transported to your last cold home—the grave. If the skin is not fed, it wrinkles. Forget the complexion and it fades. Starve the hair roots and the hair falls on the floor.

Neglect health and soon it is on crutches. Neglect nerves and they ache. Forget bones and they soften. Fail to feed the heart and soon it stops. Starve the brain and the brain cells shrink and the memory will be a blank. Breathe through the mouth and soon adenoids fill the nasal passages. Carry the arm in a sling and the muscles shrink. Fail to supply food iron and you suffer from anemia and menstrual cramps. Neglect the infant and it dies.

Leave your elegant home to wind, dirt, moisture, rain, frost, rust, bugs, and street boys, and what will become of it in

17

a few months? Leave your plates, knives and utensils to dirt, moisture and rust, and what are the results? Go to the woods and neglect yourself for a time and soon you look like a monkey!

Nature does nothing for a man beyond supplying him with raw material. He must provide himself with his own food. He has developed wheat from a weed. He has made the world habitable. He has built his own home. If anything is to be done for him, he must do it himself. If he does nothing for his brain and genius, weeds grow in his brain and bring him a crop of sorrow, fear, failure and tears.

Ambition leads to wealth, health and happiness. Drifting leads to poverty, misery, disease, suffering and tears. Look at the drifter, look at the idler, look at the tramp! What are they? Sons of God? Yes, but they have wandered away from heaven and have sold their birthright for a mess of porridge. Drifting impulses lead us downward. It is easy to drift, easy to raise weeds, easy to grow bugs. Drifting and weeds are twins of failure and sorrow. What will a sparkling genius accomplish if he permits himself to drift? We cannot develop muscles by novel reading, nor can we feed the brain with coffee, white bread and doughnuts. Personality is foreign to the idler. Nobility of soul, sainthood and piety are not found in the criminal. No loafer is equal to Abraham Lincoln. Tramps do not have gifted children. Men and women of greatness are men and women of effort and culture.

The law of healing is that we heal from within out, from the head down and in reverse order as symptoms have appeared in the body.

Just as we have built a rug, we must be prepared to unravel it, reconstruct it using our new knowledge, building it stronger and better than ever. It is necessary to recognize we must replace old thoughts and old tissue for the new. This is better in action and integrity, which you can depend upon. This is a creed you will be proud to have as you walk through life. This is quality healing.

We cannot put salve on our aches and pains and take care of symptoms anymore. We cannot use excuses. We are going to put new thought in place of old. We need something we can depend on.

If we wish to become known, popular, noble and prosperous, weeds must not grow in the brain. It must be weeded out and noble thoughts take its place. Some system of culture is needed for each man or woman of accomplishment. Bashfulness, timidity, scorn, contempt, conceit, self abasement, paltriness, abjection, cowardice, temper, haughtiness, awkwardness, bewilderment, fear of people, stage-fright, hesitation, embarrassment, faltering, stammering, despair, gloom, lack of faith in the future or in self, distrust, fear of poverty, inferiority complex, fears of every variety—what are they but brain weeds, brain spooks that must be weeded out or driven out of brain, heart and soul? Such unfavorable characteristics stand in the way of success, health, comfort, peace and happiness. Who cares for a bashful man? Can a timid man succeed? Does a man who lacks self reliance undertake anything whether he is capable or not? Is a scornful man popular? Is a paltry man influential? Is a conceited man a favorite in social circles? Is a coward offered high positions? Is a high-tempered man a pleasing companion? Is a confused, bewildered girl paid a high salary? Can a faltering, embarrassed woman make herself a success as an actress? Can a man who has a "poverty complex" make money? Can anyone whose brain is full of weeds, and negative qualities make himself a success, or can he make anyone happy? A boy or a girl, a man or a woman, with an inferiority complex is in a jail. How can she succeed, or how can he influence others favorably? She must liberate herself by a system of brain building. It is easy to drive "brain spooks" out of the brain when we know **how**. Each person owes himself some system of self culture and brain building.

In the next lesson, we will explore the art of coming into agreement with others and learning to lead them by leading ourselves first.

LESSON 2

LEARNING TO AGREE, YET LEADING

Learn to agree with others, pleasingly, yet lead them as well as yourself.

THE SECRET OF SELF TRAINING

When a noble sentiment is active in your *Great Within*, it diffuses an attraction or influence of its own. Thus, self exaltation is its own reward. Noble sentiments exalt you and those with whom you come in contact. When we are moved by noble sentiments, we can sway others and govern ourselves. Self exaltation leads to leadership, self mastery, self training, self regulation. To fill the mind with sentiments of self exaltation does the work in every case. The lower mind is like an unruly mob, but self exaltation rules, regulates, governs, sways and leads the lower mind. The higher mind is the *Great Within*, and self exaltation is the secret of unfolding the *Great Within*.

Dwelling constantly on noble thoughts and sentiments leads to leadership, self training and self discipline. The eyes, ears, feet, fingers, head, body, nerves, muscles, tongue, senses, thoughts, emotions, wishes, desires, feelings, temper impulses must be trained to act according to the higher dictates of the *Great Within*.

While traveling through India, I realized that we have two directions to go—to the outer world for happiness or we can go within. The one thing I have had drilled into me is to recognize that it is so important to see that what a man is deepest, he really is. This is where this course of training is going to do the greatest amount of good for you. We start from within and we come out. Every cell will feel every thought in your body, and if it can permeate life, you will find you live on what you pour forth. If people know what your inner feelings are and you can pour forth this nobility of self, you will find they will look to you because you are genuine. You are genuine from within out.

When the sentiment of self exaltation sways the mind, it is possible to train fingers, govern temper, direct impulses, control thoughts, suppress feelings, guide feet, bridle tongues, manage minds, regulate thoughts, discipline emotions, control passions, direct bodily movement, master and train nerves, influence conduct, command, guide and manage self and others gently, nobly, firmly. Self exaltation is the commander-in-chief of all the forces of body, mind, thought, heart and soul. When we know what self exaltation is and how to call up sentiments of self exaltation, self command is easy in any circle and among any class of people—in business offices, halls, on public platforms, in the senate, among mobs or lords, any and everywhere. No more bashfulness, no timidity, no fear, no complexes will ever bother us any more.

WHAT IS SELF EXALTATION?

Let us give an explanation in regard to self exaltation so we may know what self exaltation signifies. It means to:

Search for our own greatness until
    we find it, is to exalt ourselves;
Convince ourselves that a God actually
    dwells in our *Great Within*,
    is to exalt ourselves;
Give ourselves the self recognition
    that is due to us is to recognize
    our own high qualities;
Raise ourselves high in our own eyes;
Thrill with joy and confidence in
    ourselves;
Elevate ourselves in self estimation;

Say, as David said, "Study me, I am
fearfully and wonderfully made";
Fill our souls with sublime sentiments;
Honor ourselves;
Feel noble;
Tell ourselves that we came here
from the high heavens, that we
have a sacred mission to perform
and that we shall and will perform
it nobly;
Convince ourselves that we have a
perfect command of our every act,
thought and emotion, and that we
have perfect control over our every nerve.

It also means to:

Expand in soul and soar like the eagle
in space;
Give scope to mind, distinctness to voice,
dignity to walk, altitude to aspiration,
control to tongue, peace to soul, nobility
to purposes, direction to action, expansion
to chest, range to breathing, stillness to personality;
Trust the future;
Hope and watch for success;
Trust ourselves, if only in imagination;
Promise ourselves much and joyfully
expect it to come in the near future;
Live in a higher soul altitude;
Forget our own folly, faults, errors;
Find our higher qualities and those
of others;
Live in our higher selves and thank God
for making us as perfect as we are;
Help others to find their *Great Within*;
Feel and think that we are God-like
and made in His image;
Feel lofty;
Convince ourselves that we are masters
of every situation;

To sit like a statue of repose and
    let the world spin as we dwell on
    exalted sentiments;
Long for the communion with our higher
    selves, with God, angels, saints
    and noble living people;
Reason out our own greatness and find
    our noble qualities, convinced of the
    fact that a God lives within us,
    that our possibilities are so great
    that we have not the faintest idea
    of what is **not** possible for us.

All of the foregoing mind exercises have a tendency to exalt us. This is self exaltation. This will bring **results in each and every case.**

Therefore, give your soul wings and tell yourself that all things are possible for you. Always find your soul with sublime sentiments or self estimation. Exalt yourself in your own eyes. Raise yourself in your own eyes. When you do this you give yourself the recognition which is due to you from yourself. You are unfolding the *Great Within.* You are building brain cells and arousing sleeping brain cells by the millions. You are reconstructing yourself by the processes of self exaltation, whether you know it or not, or whether you believe it or not. Every time you read the course, you build new cells and arouse sleeping cells. **Read it often.** Self exaltation is made up of "ex," "up"; "altus," "high"; "action," "act." Thus the word means that it is the act of raising yourself high in your own estimation.

Before we start building up, we must stop breaking down, and in the following Lesson 3, we will find several valuable steps in preparing ourselves for leadership. These steps entail what to do and what not to do in exalting the *Great Within* and becoming who we truly are, leaders of men and masters of our destiny.

LESSON 3

BECOMING A SERENE AND MIGHTY LEADER

Negative states of mind result in a negative or weak personality. Positive states of mind give us a self assured, obstinate, contrary personality. Self exaltation and noble states of mind make an exalted, noble, influential personality, a still, serene, but mighty and popular leader. Recognize and be aware of the fact that all good things are coming to you because you are seeking. That which you are seeking is also seeking you.

HIGH POSITIONS AHEAD

There are high positions ahead of you if you *trust* yourself. You develop public confidence by trusting yourself. This leads to high positions.

SWAYING OTHERS WITHOUT FORCE

Under the influence of the sentiment of self exaltation, you can sway others without securing their attention first, and without exercising a steady intention to accomplish that which you wish. Self exaltation is noble, for it permits you. You have probably been trying to live without this important commander-in-chief or without the soul's spirit of leadership.

HOW NOBLE THOUGHTS ENNOBLE

Noble thoughts ennoble the soul and yield a higher soul altitude, greater opportunities, a greater brain capacity. It is impossible to think noble thoughts without ennobling ourselves. Small-minded men act in the lower spheres, whether they have university degrees or not, or whether they are born of kings or counts or whether they are millionaires or paupers.

SEEK NOBLE ASSOCIATES

High-minded associates arouse your higher-soul qualities. They develop qualities of nobility in you as well as in them. Your soul expands and you become magnanimous in their presence. Select noble associates always.

It is not to say we must "pick" out the people that we associate with. You will find there are times for the development of your deepest self that you must "pick" out the people that will help to exalt you. Those that you know you feel at home with, you can eat with and feel happy with. It is very necessary to take the higher road in life. The higher road is one that is going to lead you to even higher paths as you go onto the higher altitudes.

FEEDING THE BRAIN

Live close to the vegetable kingdom, the garden, the orchard, and depend upon animal phosphorus, animal lecithin, animal albumin for the feeding of your brain, and you need not know much more about diets and health foods.

HOW NERVE FORCE IS LOST

Keep your skin dry and warm or nerve force and animal heat are lost. Muscular electricity in the body is lost by radiation and convection. Sudden turns and stops, vehement feelings, passions and states of mind destroy self composure and nerve force. But self contentment favors self mastery. It is necessary to realize that God approves of a good body as well as He approves of a good mind and proper spiritual attitude. We travel the path we believe God approves.

PREVENTING NERVE STORMS

Attitudes of mental repose develop nerve trunks and spinal ganglia. Such mind attitudes of repose are possible under the influence of self exaltation. It overcomes nervousness and nerve storms.

REACHING—THE NERVE EXERCISES

Slow increase and decrease of nerve tension enlarge the storehouses of nervous energy. Tension and relaxation of nerves should always be slow and gradual. Clinch your fist slowly and increasingly until it is as hard as iron. Then relax the force in your fist slowly and decreasingly and you know what we mean by graduated nerve tension. All nerve exercises should be done as I have described here.

CARRIAGE THAT EUROPEAN NOBLES ADMIRE

A correct carriage requires a full chest, lungs full of air and upright position of the body in sitting and walking, also active sentiments of self exaltation. This gives us that autonomic deportment so admired by those of noble heritage and sentiment.

THE BEST NERVE SLEEP

If you stay up at night to ten, eleven, twelve one o'clock, you pay a heavy bill later in life. The best nerve sleep or nerve rest is before twelve o'clock at night. Therefore, retire early.

NERVE REST AND RELAXATION FOR THE NERVOUS

This is an exercise. Sit down in the evening several hours after eating and inhale and exhale as usual, but holding breath just a little longer and exhaling slightly slower than usual. Keep this up for fifteen minutes, paying attention to nothing but your own breath as it moves up and down in your chest, focusing at the same time upon your exalted, heavenly origin. You will be surprised at your mental self composure. All nervousness has left you and perfect nerve calm prevails.

WHAT NEURO-STATIC EXERCISES DO FOR THE NERVOUS

Neuro-static exercises are still exercises. They develop nerve control, finger and tongue control. Stormy temperaments require such exercises, under the influence of the sentiment of self exaltation. They also need the magnesium food element contained in yellow corn-bran broth and in other foods.

AVOID UNNECESSARY DRUGS

When God made Adam and Eve, He created no drugstore. There were no can openers in the Garden of Eden. There were no French cooks. The doctor's drugs should seldom enter your sanctuary; food is man's best medicine.

We have to be careful as we go through life that we attract the very finest. Remember always that the body is a servant to the mind and the spirit. Remember also that the environment helps to mold our body and build it or it will help to destroy it. The only medicine we should use is that which comes from God's garden. Many feel they have to go on a trip or they have missed something. They bring on sympathy for themselves. Sympathy is like a floating cloud. We cannot lean on it or draw from it. We cannot grow from it. We need knowledge, wisdom and guidance.

WHAT TO AVOID

Temper, like electricity in the clouds, thunders and destroys itself. Temper is closely related to insanity. A high-tempered man lacks brain and judgment "when his steam is up." Temper goes through the nerves like an explosion. It dries up the nerves like a dry, hot wind in the desert. Temper, like gossip, makes enemies as fast as it rains in Seattle in December. Cynicism is like a fierce owl, hooting in an icy forest on a cold, dark night. Leave high-tempered people, cynics, gossipers and fools to themselves as long as you unfold your *Great Within*. Worry, grief, sorrow and disappointment eat at the vitals like cancer. Develop a high-minded indifference and nothing can reach your heart and soul.

A NATURAL BEAUTIFIER

Loss of sleep is destructive to nerves and brain cells. It dries up the brain fluid, sets the nerves on edge and acts on the brain like angry nettles. Sleep preserves grace, beauty and complexion in all people who are not largest at the midriff, or live on a high calorie diet and have a sweet tooth.

In Lesson 4, we learn the importance of maintaining proper nerve force and about the different temperament types.

Each person is an individual type, and must take care to develop the brain centers that enhance his or her particular temperament.

LESSON 4

AN EXCELLENT SPOT FOR A VACATION

Extreme sultry summer heat weakens nerves and brain. Take a vacation during the sultry days of July and August to some cool spot, as for instance, Oakland, California, and adopt a cooling diet high in formic, citric, tartaric, tannic and phosphoric acids.

THE SEATS OF THE HEAT CENTERS; HOW TO PROTECT THEM

The heat centers of the body should be protected with silk, fur or both. These centers are located in the upper spine, the small of the back, the neck, ankles, wrists and the iliac section of the lower abdomen. We must keep the ankles of growing children warm, especially when children are growing. Wearing red socks during the day can help you have warm feet at night so sleeping can be more complete. It is well to recognize what color can do for you. Too much red can be too stimulating to the sexual system, to blood pressure, to stress and strain. Blue may be a tranquilizer in your life. Many need green around them; orange for the nerves. Color therapy is one of the things we could lean on and get a lot of good for ourselves. It can be a protective thing in our life, and it can also be one of the things to bring more happiness than you could ever imagine. Study color, vibrations, music, God and nature.

Everyone is trying to overcome acid conditions that are produced in our bodies. Acids are produced in busy bodies. We have to learn what it is to rest, to go silent, to sit on a rock, have quiet times in life, when we can recuperate and let the rest of the world go by. To let go and let our higher self take over is really the great thing in meditation.

OVERCOMING BASHFULNESS FOREVER

Self-exalted states of mind overcome bashfulness forever.

THE HIGHEST TEST OF NERVE FORCE

Internal brain force and nerve force externally controlled, directed and regulated is the highest test of nerve force, self training and self mastery, whether in private or public. By "externally controlled," I mean subject to rationally determined goals.

A REFINED EXTERIOR; HOW DEVELOPED

Graceful self assurance and delicacy of technique develop a graceful deportment and a refined exterior by calling out the artistic side of man. This overcomes awkwardness and rough, unpracticed manners. Practice makes perfect, as they say.

CORRECT BREATHING

The diaphragmatic method of breathing with ample range, when the mind is moved by exalted sentiments, calms the nerves and attracts the blood to the autonomic brain centers. It builds new cells, arouses sleeping brain cells and builds up the strength of the faculty center.

THE SOUL'S COMMANDER-IN-CHIEF

Tranquility of mind, stillness of nerves and bodily members, perfect control of internal energy, train mind and nerve until all obey the dictates of that commander-in-chief that dwells in our *Great Within.*

HOW TO INCREASE NERVE FORCE

Reading at night, sighing, thumping with the feet, tapping with the fingers, whistling, humming, rocking up and down on your feet, swinging, dancing, jumping, hopping, squirming, sputtering, blowing and all sorts of useless motions should be avoided. When the body, mind, tongue and nerves are not employed in useful work, they should be in repose. Each motion, gesture, movement, thought and act uses up vitality, nerve force and brain force. Nerve force should be conserved. Brain force should be increased. Physical energy should be regulated.

Vitality should be augmented, and the ganglionic centers should be amplified. Conservation of energy is imperative in all important people. The more capital a business man has in reserve, the safer his business. Likewise, the more power we have in reserve, the more we can accomplish. We must take ourselves in charge and engineer our forces to the best advantage.

It is well that we recognize our body has many departments of reserve, ready for us to call on them. We find that the chemicals are being deposited in all of the different departments of the body. Don't wear out; don't become burned out. Don't go to the extremes in any regard. Going to bed "dog tired" is going to bed too late. Don't go to bed with a lot of your troubles. Write them down with the idea that this is the time to take care of "me." Take care of yourself fresh in the morning. Just like you can expect the best work from your horse when you attach him to the plow, which is first thing in the morning. To attach that horse to the plow after he has done a day's work, and expect the best work to come from that horse is an impossibility. We must work when we are rested.

Every organ represents a reserve for materials you can bank on. When in need, such as any experience may take out of you on an overtime job, extra effort, extra extension of your very self. Always carry a good reserve and never use up the reserve to the extreme so there is nothing left.

EXERCISE STATIC

Try once to stand like a statue of repose for two to ten minutes, holding feet, fingers, hands, arms, head, eyelids perfectly still, your mind in repose, and your bodily members will gradually learn to obey the dictates of the soul's commander-in-chief. Learn to hold your eyes still and your gaze will be steady in the presence of others. Stillness develops nerve control and the coolest faculty of the mind. Take exercises of repose every day and develop self composure.

IMPORTANT INFORMATION

Quick inhalations and exhalations with knee-bending exercises or nerve-tension exercises, seem to force the sluggish venous blood to the liver and lungs and give impulse to throat, neck and base of brain. Sluggish venous blood is often the cause of many ailments. Do this exercise often.

When we have any venous congestion in the body that is toxic, sluggish, slow-moving blood, it may be necessary for us to get ourselves into action. We need to supply the blood with plenty of iron so we attract all of the oxygen needed by the tissues. Iron and oxygen are the two "frisky horses" that give the energy and power to overcome, and to develop the best body. Be sure we have enough exercise to move the old blood out of the venous structures. Invite the new arterial blood into our tissues, so we may have good repair, a good body and a good mind all working together.

Everyone should keep themselves in good mental balance. No one should go to extremes. Extremes do not have balance. We can wear out mental suggestions. The physical body may be given more to care for than it possibly can protect from mental processes that break down our physical self.

WHAT PHLEGMATIC PEOPLE SHOULD DO

Sluggish temperaments require tension exercises. When nerve force is increased from laxity to tensity, and decreased by degrees from tensity to laxity, we reach the nerves and develop greater force. The nerves are strengthened, electricity set free, power generated and fresh blood flows more freely to brain and tissues.

ANALYZING YOUR TEMPERAMENT

Types and temperaments should be understood in all systems of development. Types and temperaments can be divided into:

Apathetic types or temperaments
Passive types
Impulsive temperaments
Positive types of people
Harmonious temperaments
Intensive temperaments.

Apathetic, indifferent, passive and phlegmatic people must be aroused; must be recharged. They require dynamic tension exercises, stimulating foods, high altitudes, vigorous breathing, even irritative, mental suggestions to arouse them. Impulsive people are emotional, sudden, interruptive, wavering. They need static exercises. Suggestions to them are useless, for they have a hundred mental changes per hop. Their thoughts are like jumping jacks. Static exercises are better for them. Impulsive people should be trained to stillness and repose.

34

Positive people require friendly, amicable, loving, respectful, kind suggestions and gentle exercises. They should develop the social areas in the brain at the same time the autonomic center is developed.

Intensive temperaments should be trained the same as positive people, except they require neuro-static exercises. Intense people go to excess and use up their life force too rapidly. They must be held back as a wild horse.

Harmonious people can be given all sorts of exercises and ennobling suggestions.

Weak, ailing people require gentle training and easy exercises.

Children from seven to ten years of age can seldom be trained, until later on.

Some children can start with this course of training very early. Others require time to realize it is necessary. Still others have to develop a desire. There are those who are ready and want the new development as soon as possible. This is unusual, but children, as a rule, can be taken care of through influence rather than teaching. Children are strongly influenced by the parents' example.

So-called "brain breathing" is dangerous and stupid, for we cannot force air into the brain by any methods of exercise. The brain receives its oxygen supply through the blood. Oxygen can be increased in the blood by aerobic exercise; it cannot be "forced" into brain cells any faster than the brain's metabolic limit. At best, we utilize only four percent of the air we breathe. Ninety-six percent of the air we breathe is lost.

ALL OBEY THE LEADER—AUTONOMIA

When temperaments and dispositions are understood, we can use common sense in our systems of culture.

A controlled voice, under the influence of the sentiment of self exaltation, impresses children, mates, pupils, servants, students, judges, juries, witnesses, customers, friends, audiences, people at large and ourselves, to obedience. Excitement, weakness, negativeness, bashfulness and force defeat us. There is only one faculty of mind that impels to *self-imposed* obedience. Force can force people to obey; reason can reason people into obedience; fear can terrify and intimidate; hypnotism can annihilate mind and personality; temptation, allurement, seduction, persuasion, fair speech, artifices, etc., can be used to lure, entice, seduce or inveigle others, as well as ourselves, into acts to which the *Great Within* objects. Such means are ignoble. Noble self-imposed obedience to the dictates of noble characters or to the dictates of the *Great Within* is the only kind of obedience that is genuine and noble.

All faculties and people obey the self-management faculty—the true sense of pride and nobility faculty. It is also called the regal or leadership center. It is the development of this faculty that qualifies us for self mastery, self management, and gives us a true sense of our own self hood. It gives us what universities cannot give—a Self-Conferred Diploma of Leadership.

Autonomy means self government through self law. The audacious rebel, the bold lawyer, the impudent knave, the self-assured pugilist, the intrepid general, the presumptuous employer, the mutinous mob, the rebellious boy, all fall in line and obey the leader. We could not disobey a true leader if we tried. Under forced obedience, we become fools or tools. When **autonomia** governs the *Great Within*, mind, faculties, impulses, thoughts, emotions, fingers, feet, gestures, utterances, laughter, eyes, senses, nerves, muscles also obey the inner man, the commander-in-chief of all the forces, powers and equipment we possess. This is why we should develop this important faculty diligently and religiously. It is the weakest faculty that people have; it should be the strongest. Self exaltation develops it without fail.

This is one center we must pay the greatest attention to, because this is the center where we have a true sense of pride, nobility, leadership and self exaltation, not conceit, nor that kind of sense nobility that motivates haughty monarchs, despotic lords, vain society women and wealthy monopolists who are purse proud. We do not call any such characteristics pride. We call pride by its right name, self conceit, despotism, vanity, greed, haughtiness. We find that this particular center has no such "pride" in its function. This center is not proud because of a big stomach, nor because of wealth, title, standing or possessions, but because of its own native sense of self hood.

This faculty gives us a sense of soul altitude. It lifts us to higher heights. It exalts and ennobles us. It fills the soul with serene loftiness and enables us to think high thoughts and do noble deeds, to live in our higher selves, to rule, govern, lead and to help others to higher positions. It is this faculty that ennobles us to find our own superior qualities.

We develop a personality for our *Great Within*, our sacred self hood, our nobler selves, our soul greatness, our own genius. We develop the mastery of self, of leadership and a whole array of passions, appetites and tendencies. It is the sole genius of self leadership. When it is weak, the sole republic has no leader. This center enables us to save our nerve force until it is needed. It bridles our tongues, directs the senses, sways the faculties and guides the thoughts by sentiments of soul elevation and exaltation.

The leader lives in a lofty elevation and exaltation. The leader lives in a lofty soul attitude rather, with all of his faculties. This is why he is a leader.

If he lives in the basement of soul and brain, or if he lives in the abdomen, or in the purse, he is not a leader in the soul republic nor anywhere else. Every faculty, tendency, wish, passion and emotion, yields to this faculty, and people, white and black, old and young, rich and poor, mighty and common, mobs, warriors, servers and executives yield to it because it is the leader when it predominates. It enables us to commune with our higher selves and enables us to know what we are. This one faculty widens the soul's horizons. It enables us to live above our surroundings and our higher soul attitudes.

Thus, we are masters of ourselves and leaders of men. It gives us what universities cannot give, a self-conferred diploma of leadership without giving it and without knowing it.

This faculty extols others in our eyes, while self aggrandizement tries to climb up by pulling others down. It is the spirit of leadership that thinks noble thoughts. It is always gentle, noiseless and self composed, searching for the soul's highest qualities. It never boasts. It forgets self. It feels no need of self recommendation, self idolatry and self praise. It is self contentment itself.

This faculty has an imposing stride in our walk and makes us feel as serene as a landscape in May. It craves no friends, no exciting entertainment, for it is its own fulfillment; its own master; its own leader; and can enjoy its own sacred presence. It fills our souls with an exalted sentiment of peace and lofty tranquility; a soul serenity that knows no nervousness, even in battle and panic. People's criticism, flattery or praise are like flattened bullets at its feet. It soars like an eagle in space and poisoned arrows and defamation cannot reach it in its soul attitude of magnanimity. It is its own law, its own master, its own wholeness, its own leader and a dignified leader of the people without knowing it or thinking self greater because of it.

It soars in the higher spheres of the people, and people feel there is something *great*, noble and super eminent about this faculty. It makes us feel fearfully and wonderfully made and willing to thank the Almighty for His genius in making us so wonderful.

This faculty makes us think of our high mission in life, our heavenly rank. Our exalted self hood, high birth, high aims, noble purposes, elevated sentiment and nearness to God, the most high. While it is not a spiritual faculty, it is nevertheless dominated with sentiments of loftiness and self exaltation not common to other soul faculties. The principle function of this is to lead and govern self in the first place, and to throw a certain degree of control over others when an opportunity offers itself. There is nothing for popularity, worship or officialism, nor for official functions or red tape. Its main function centers in self leadership and self contentment.

This faculty impels to obedience. It falls into line instinctively without fuss, bluster, threats and force. The impulses from this faculty are governed, not by persuasion, threats, force, legal authority, reason, judgement and so forth, but by that same dignity or spirit of leadership. This is what that solemn soul leader is qualified to do easily, quietly, silently, honorably, dignifiedly, mastered in such a way that there would be no complaint or rebellion, sedition or unpleasantness in the mind or outside of the mind. All listen to and obey the voice of this faculty. There is something mysterious, supernatural, even preternatural about this faculty, its voice and serene commands. We cannot resist its voice and request. We obey instinctively, willingly, happily, and feel as if we have been elevated to a higher altitude, high above our own selves by hearing and obeying the voice of this faculty.

A manly conduct is the effect of strong and active faculties such as this. We can keep the body erect and the body organs in position under its influence, but not otherwise. This is what is meant by walking the upright man. It gives us perfectly dignified ease with manners. An air of loftiness, a real sense of distinction and self confidence are born of it. This sentiment of self respect springs from it. It gives a commanding tone to our voice. It enables us to keep our good behavior, inspires public confidence and leads to exalted position. It is the spirit of aristocratic genetics or sense of noble birth, a sense of self hood. It is a sense of self importance, a sense of self nobility. It enables us to relax mind and nerves. This faculty leads people to their true selves, to their own options and places. Out of it develops an independence of action and a liberty of individual interests. It gives us all freedom of action. It is royal-minded and does not rob us of our independence, freedom and liberty.

This faculty is needed in all true leaders. A boss is a domineering individual, but a leader is not. All faculties are willing and glad to honor the leader, if he is a leader. Even the boss yields to the leader without murmur. It is the true spirit of leadership. It is never discommoded, not even before kings, lords and gods. It acts trustfully in a noble manner and never loses self possession at any time. It makes us obey, no matter how disobedient we may otherwise be, nor does it matter whether we are in beggars' attire or in kingly uniform. This faculty really means self government through self law. A personal magnetism is developed that none can resist. It is elective and selective as an influence. He can always enforce his authority without enforcing by force.

It makes a continuous calm, soul serene, temper placid, exterior reposeful. It produces an unmistakable stillness of body, mind and nerves, and a remarkably noble and serene composure. It makes the nerves restful.

It soars high without trying. It enables us to forget our faults and live in higher selves. It gives us a keen sense of our high origin, yet we never boast or talk about ourselves. We are simply self satisfied. We never impress the people with our importance. A really important man never really blows his own trumpet. He acts independently and noble.

When this faculty is weak, we become public in power, uneasy, timid, restless, perhaps bashful and likely to suffer from stage fright. When this faculty is weak, it cannot act, move, speak, gesticulate and appear differently than we are. We have it to give us self composure, the command accent of pitch and vocal expression, that exalted personality. When this faculty is weak, we find that we cannot command ourselves. It is difficult to make ourselves obey, our children to obey us, other people to obey, mobs, audiences, sinners, criminals, executives and so forth. They may obey us when we use persuasion, temper, violence, law, force to make others obey, but such measures are mob measures.

This center has to have the proper blood supply, nerve supply, calculation, otherwise inflammation in these areas can lead a person to serious mental problems.

In our next lesson—Lesson 5—we will learn how to apply the leadership that emerges from the process of self exaltation by influencing audiences favorably. Without followers, there are no leaders, and without knowledge of how to sway listeners, all leadership is pointless. Read and reread each lesson to get the most from it.

Dennis Weaver is one whom I admire for his inner growth and development of self.

LESSON 5

HOW TO SWAY AUDIENCES

That faculty (soul power or emotion) which is active in you when you meet someone or appear before the public, determines the influence you exert over yourself, over others or both. If you are bashful, your case is lost.

An able graduate student was to preach a sermon with Luther behind him on the platform. As a text, the student commenced: "I am the good shepherd." He became stage struck and his tongue paralyzed. Luther caught hold of the student's coat tail and whispered, "You may be a good sheep, but you are not a good shepherd."

If you feel great, noble, exalted; if you take a strong position; if you carry a chest filled with air; if your mind is charged with internal life; if your eyes are steady, warm and glowing; if your voice is controlled; if your sentiment of self exaltation is soaring and your soul peaceful; if you begin slowly and fill your lungs with air as you proceed; then if you will think of your exalted, birth and your great mission in life, you will present a powerful message with noble sentiments and irresistible appeal. You will look like a man, orate like a Demosthenes and influence audiences like an Ingersol, because you will have command of your own faculties, your own knowledge, your own vocabulary and your own reason. But as long as you think about yourself, you will be a sheep and a failure both, whatever you may know or whatever your titles may be. It does not depend upon what we know, but rather upon how we feel.

Lessons in oratory bring us nowhere, but self exaltation brings us to the front. Learned professors and trained orators often look like educated monkeys. They assume unmanly attitudes. We look as we feel. Universities train us intellectually but know nothing about the soul's function nor about types, diets and brain building.

"WE ARE FEARFULLY AND WONDERFULLY MADE"

Lofty, exalted exclusiveness is peculiar to nature's real nobleman. He practices in privacy. This is what you should do. Let your exercises be known to yourself only. Let no one see this course. Let it be sacred. Let no one read it nor know what you are doing. Become select and exclusive. No thought, no act, no man, woman, child, angel or God is sacred to the familiar man (although each man, each woman is "fearfully and wonderfully made"). The self-exalted man feels that everything is sacred. He sees God in each blade of grass, in each atom and orb, in each woman, child and man, himself included. God, angels, saints and divines are exalted, noble, great, mighty, always civil, gentle, kind, composed. If we have any respect for God, we must acknowledge that He did a mighty work when He created us, and that we are"fearfully and wonderfully made."

BECOMING A LEADER

Self regulation trains the leader and develops the spirit of leadership. The leader is a self regulator. He prescribes rules for himself and follows those rules. He is a system maker. He rules himself and has perfect command of fingers, feet, nerves and faculties. He obeys his own rules and regulations. He is a law to himself. Leadership begins with self. The world is full of servers, bosses, straw bosses, rulers, dogmatists, greedy politicians, loafers, followers, and tramps, but it lacks leaders. Lead yourself first and soon you will lead others. Prescribe rules for others. Leaders are well paid; bosses are paid fairly well; drivers of men receive a fair wage; servers are poorly paid; followers, loafers and tramps are usually poor. **Be a leader!**

METHODS OF SELF TRAINING

Neuro-static exercises train the nerves. Such exercises favor intense temperaments and train the nerves, fingers, feet, eyes, thoughts and senses. They develop self composure, tongue control, finger control, thought control, nerve control, and save brain force, health and vitality.

EXERTING A NOBLE INFLUENCE

Stand about five feet or more away from the person to whom you talk; look him into the eyes; fill your chest with air and your mind with lofty, exalted sentiments; feel that you are great and mighty; let your man sit while you stand; talk and reason steadily, consecutively, rationally and you win.

EXALTED INDEPENDENCE

Make yourself scarce among people, but always be courteous to all, whether high, low, learned, ignorant, rich, poor, old, white, black or green, native or foreigner. The leader is an exalted personality. He is seldom seen, seldom heard. He governs through others. He is master of all. Develop leadership and you will advance. People will come to you instead of your going to them and applying for positions. You will have a business and an income of your own.

YOUR INFINITE POSSIBILITIES

Each man is capable of infinite possibilities. Each man is a collection of cells that run into billions. In proportion, as we train, develop, regulate, direct and unfold our energies in that exact proportion, we will succeed on a larger and larger scale.

It is not what we know or do that success depends upon, but rather upon *how we use* that which we know, also upon what we leave alone. The difference between an exalted man and a man of failure is that the exalted man leaves alone such acts that the man of failure commits every minute of the day. The man of failure is always a scatterbrain.

WHAT POPULARITY AND SUCCESS DEPEND UPON

If people believe in us, we succeed whether we have faith in ourselves or not. But people have no faith in us if we have no faith in ourselves. We need not think that people worship us even if they believe in us. Nor does it matter. Why should people worship us? We should be exalted in mind, noble in sentiments, collected in thoughts, consecutive in reasoning, honest in motive, honorable in action, stately in carriage, free and easy in manner and always have a noble purpose in view, whether people believe in us or not. Otherwise, we defeat ourselves, baffle our motives, degrade our personality, lower our talent, lose our influence and meet failure instead of success. No matter how much people believe in us, they will not patronize us after they find out that we are dishonest, ignoble, unreliable.

Even if people believe in us and make us prosperous for a time, that success will be of short duration when they find out that we cannot be trusted. We should never give people unpleasant suggestions, never dwell upon their faults, never depreciate them, never undermine their plans, never talk ill about them, but always dwell on their good qualities and they are willing to make us prosperous.

It is a rather sad fact that people have more faith in others than in themselves. Hence, people are servers and their own slaves. This lack of self trust hinders them from doing their best. When we mistrust ourselves, we lower our talent; we sink. But when we elevate ourselves in self estimation, search for our own greatness, live in sublime sentiments of self exaltation, thrill with joy and self confidence, recognize our own high qualities—we increase talent, worth, honor, integrity, genius and nobility. This gives us greater and greater influence through public patronage or through personal enterprises or both. To wish, dare, act, to trust our plans and act on them, to gratify noble desires, to start an enterprise and daringly, diligently, devotedly, patiently, trustfully, efficiently, nobly and energetically work for the same—*always* leads to success. Aspiration should not be crushed. Talent should not be hidden under a bushel. Good thoughts should not be uprooted when they are but tender plants. To desire influence, fame, health, wealth, power, position, learning is desirable, providing we use all for noble ends.

As we think, so we are; and as we think of ourselves, so will we appear to ourselves and others. In Lesson 6, we will learn how important it is to use our thoughts and sentiments to build our brain power and contribute to the process of self exaltation.

Walls and fences separate people. It is hard to realize the value of the Great Within when we imprison ourselves with our thinking.

LESSON 6

THOUGHTS AND SENTIMENTS AS BRAIN BUILDERS

Search for your own higher qualities, find your higher self and you become great in proportion. Every person has a *Great Within*, power asleep, genius latent, possibilities slumbering, gifts undiscovered, aptitudes unfolded. *Each person needs a self introduction.* Self recognition is imperative.

Man does not know himself. He is more than he knows. Exalt people in their own eyes, and you become popular and influential whether you want to be or not. Find your own higher qualities and you become great in your own eyes. Feel exalted and you become exalted. It all depends upon how we feel. Feel great and you become greater. Feel exalted and you become more exalted. Feel noble and you ennoble yourself. Feel honest and you grow in honesty. Feel bashful and you look like a sheep, act like one and talk like one. But dwell upon your great mission in life, exalt yourself in your own eyes and bashfulness evaporates like smoke, nor do you know what has become of it. Sentiments and thoughts are cell builders, brain builders, soul builders. What you put your attention to grows.

You may just as well dwell upon your own greatness as upon your own littleness. Imagination is constructive, for it is faculties at work in your *Great Within*. If you lack courage, imagine a few times each day that you are a courageous person, that you can meet anyone, the devil included, and in about a year, you will be courageous.

CONSERVING AND USING YOUR
SELF-PROTECTIVE FORCES

Save your nerve force until you need it. Temper, arguments, reading, studies, dissipation, dances, cinemas, talk, worry, strife, anxiety, emotions, gestures, jumping, etc., use up your mental and physical energy. When nerve force is not used nobly and usefully, it should be stored away in the nerve batteries. This will make you greater, useful, popular, more composed, mightier, nobler.

Never look people and animals into the eyes unnecessarily, but hold your mind and nerves tense, lungs full of air and dwell upon your godlike qualities. If you do that, no man, no woman, no animal, no snake can have have any influence on you. If you ever feel unable to use your own forces, you are controlled by hidden forces. That is the time you should dwell on your own greatness, fill your lungs with air, tense your fists, nerves and muscles, call up exalted thoughts, commune with your God who dwells in your *Great Within*, and no power on Earth, no hidden forces in the sky, can influence you, no schemer can make you buy, intimidate you, nor coerce you to sign any documents.

CLOSE ATTENTION OF GREAT VALUE

Let not your thoughts drift. Pay attention to every act, move, gesture, expression, and pay close attention to the acts and speech of other people.

DISCOVERING YOUR OWN GENIUS

Be your own company. Learn to value *your own sacred self hood;* it is the highest, noblest power you possess. Never stay long with others. Be your own companion as long as you are building brain cells in the *Great Within*. Every man has genius slumbering within. To discover it is one's greatest mission.

By brain building under the influence of exalted sentiments, you can add millions of brain cells, increase in genius and influence every day that passes by. You can use your energies to greater advantage. It gives you a new aim, a higher ideal, a new hope, a new lease on life. It is the greatest health insurance you can get, and it will cost nothing. It opens up new avenues to soul and brain. It makes you better appreciated by yourself and will give you greater public recognition and self recognition. It will give you superior self control, finger control, thought control, functional control, a stately carriage, a cultured exterior, a more reposeful personality. It will give you a self introduction and prepare you for greater deeds, also for the great hereafter, which is best of all.

It may be true that you cannot reconstruct yourself all at once, but all of the time you are *recharging* yourself and constantly eradicating negative qualities and making yourself greater, stronger, nobler. You are in your own university. You are your own teacher, disciplinarian, your own law. You are in the School of Leadership studying a subject that no school, college, university, professor, minister of the gospel in the world can teach you. In the course of time, as you go on with this system of *self culture,* your sleeping genius will unfold, awaken and become active on a larger and larger scale.

A SELF INTRODUCTION TO YOUR HIGHER SELF; KNOW THYSELF

How will you, we or others know us as we really are? Self exaltation does the work unknowingly in us. It builds brain cells and brain centers on a larger pattern. When this is done, you will know yourself or anyone will know himself as he never before did. This increases genius, facilitates concentration, increases effort, augments efficiency and qualifies you to achieve more, to advance, to occupy higher positions, to increase your bank account.

TALK TO YOUR SELF AS FOLLOWS:
MONOLOGUE—VOICE PRACTICE

Now, I unfold my *Great Within*. It is of greatest importance that I think high thoughts of myself. I cultivate the sentiment of self exaltation. I feel like an eagle in space, lifted high above all worldly interest. I think lofty noble thoughts. I soar in imagination. I build air castles. I give my soul wings. I attend to my own affairs and let other people attend to their business. I systematize my operations, plan my own work, act under the conviction that I am heaven bred, that my mission in life is as important as I am important, that I came here to lead, govern and prepare myself for exalted offices. I keep my own affairs to myself.

I never talk much, only listen and look wise, whether I am wise or not. I am in training; I aim high, associate with superior people, act like a lord and feel like a lord. I speak in a subdued, distinct voice. I never get excited. I feel as if nothing can reach me. I am somewhat indifferent to happenings, accidents, explosions, calamities. Nothing alarms me, nothing disturbs me, nothing ruffles my temper, nothing shakes my nerves. I am ever serene.

My actions are ever controlled. I am ready for action, turmoil, trouble, insults, panic, struggle, temptations, storms, uproar, commotions, poverty, sickness, death, war, difficulties, criticism, opposition, argumentation, trials, lawsuits, afflictions and what not. Best of all, I am above all and nothing can reach me, nothing can disturb my serenity. I am as placid and serene as a smiling landscape in May.

ENGLAND—I AM KING OF ME

If I am poor, I am the same reposeful person. If my home, clothes, station in life, position, education and advantages in life are inferior, what do I care? I am the same exalted, serene, reposeful and noble person. I do not depend for my greatness on equipage, titles, position, rank, education, wealth, strength, dress, beauty, reputation, advantages, nor do I depend upon kings and lords. People can take away all of that and I am the same high-minded, great and noble person. For my greatness *is in myself, and I feel it and know it.*

I remember a friend of mine at one time was asked to make a speech. When he came to the gathering, he had not put his tie on. He had not even thought of putting one on. Upon arriving, he was told it was necessary to have a tie, so they would loan him one. He took his shirt off and put the tie on and came out to give his speech. He had done what he was told, he had his tie on while making the speech.

I am self satisfied, self composed, self content, whatever I have or have not. No restlessness for me, no nervousness, discontent, regret, bashfulness, fear, fuss, fretting, gossip, no temper, argument, nothing but serenity of mind. I compare myself with no one, but I feel that "I am fearfully and wonderfully made."

I thank God, the Great World Builder, that He made me as I am. I enjoy my own presence and can be my own companion. I can commune with myself in the stillness of the evening and thrill with joy when I dwell on my great qualities and live in my *Great Within.* I am a leader and crave no one to humor me, no one to amuse me, advise me, direct, encourage, praise or flatter me. I am self contained, the fullness of my own life. My life is as serene as my soul is tranquil.

KEEP MY OWN COUNSEL

I have no regrets in regard to the past, no worry about the future, no ill will towards anyone. I know the business of no one, nor do I want to know. If others belittle themselves, it is their business, but *my business is to be my own keeper,* my own engineer. When people become angry, I look and say nothing. If they insult me, I stand like a statue before them. Neither anger nor abuse can reach me for I soar so high that nothing can reach me. Even if it could reach me, what do I care? I accept neither praise, blame, insults nor flattery from the people. I am above all. My determination is to find the good qualities in other people and lift humanity to a higher plane. I am the same even-minded, reposeful, exalted person whatever happens.

I cannot fail, for I recognize no failure. I am happy and serene. No shadow for me. I turn failure into success; I am master of my own destiny. I soar in soul and sentiment. No one knows what I am doing. I am self collected and my affairs are self affairs. I am a commander of myself. I develop the spirit of self control, autonomy, self composure, nobility and leadership. I am developing my own brain by thought practices. It may be true that I cannot yet feel exalted and heaven bred, but I am training, developing and opening up new avenues of genius and talent through processes of cell building. If I cannot feel exalted in reality, I can at least develop my imagination. I know that imagination is nothing but faculties at work, and that all greatness is the result of cell building and effort.

We must recognize that many of us will have experiences. Never do the same experiences come to each of us that come to other people. We interpret experiences according to what we have studied, people we have met and how we think about our experiences. It comes to the place where we must realize experiences come to us for a purpose. This is examination time. This is when we pull together all we know. This is the time when we use experiences as stepping stones. There are no stumbling blocks in life.

WE WILL BE MEASURED BY OUR ENDEAVORS

This is how you should talk, feel, think and reason. Hundreds of men have elevated themselves to exalted positions, won fame and distinction in their chosen line. Go ahead with this course of self culture, and you will know yourself as you never did before. At first you cannot believe in your own assertions nor act upon them, but be patient and persevere. For if you could believe, think, feel as outlined, you would not need this course. And when you can feel as outlined, you need the course no longer. It has done its work.

SELF-NEGLECT—SINNING
AGAINST OUR NOBLER SELVES

The idea is that you should always search for your great qualities, never your inferior qualities. For instance, if you constantly affirm your inferior qualities, that is what you will reveal to others. Avoid the following kinds of thoughts: "I am timid, nervous, delicate. I have no opportunities in life, no education. I have this defect. I am sickly, bashful, self conscious, sensitive, good-for-nothing. I wish I would die. I am so poorly dressed, so homely, so fat, or so lean, I do not look right. I do not understand why I was born into this miserable world. I lack courage. My memory is so poor I cannot remember anything. I did a foolish act here, I lost nerve there, I was stupid in this place and embarrassed in that. I am bow-legged, my eyesight is poor, people are making fun of me and everybody sees my defects."

There are times when you actually know people want to throw tomatoes at you. If they want to boo you, they want to lower you to their level of consciousness. It takes a mighty strong person to stand against those tomatoes. There is one thing you should know, and it is part of the great teachings. That is, if you don't want any tomatoes thrown at you, you must get back into the crowd again.

DEATH WISH STARTED

If you thus talk, think and feel, year in and year out, what will become of you at last? Do you realize that you are constantly dwelling on your inferior qualities, and that by so doing, your brain cells shrink and die and you are tearing down your higher, nobler self? *This must be stopped forever!*

TAKE THE HIGHER PATH

To reverse this undesirable and self-destructive process, you must turn and take the higher path, the path to self exaltation. In the next lesson, we will see how self promotion leads through the rocky shoals of deception, disadvantages of the past and false exaltation to the true progress the soul of man seeks.

Dr. Jensen with the King of Hunza. Know that we can finally become the king or queen of our individual self, for a man is measured by what he is deepest.

LESSON 7

SELF PROMOTION

Self exaltation means self promotion. To do great things, accomplish mighty deeds, you should think lofty thoughts and dwell on exalted sentiments, either in imagination or in reality, to bring about great results. To raise self to a high soul altitude; to give scope to mind, thoughts, sentiments, aspirations and deeds—leads to self promotion. Faith in self is born of self exaltation. Filling your soul with serene delight in self because of noble sentiments and deeds, feeds the imagination and attracts blood to the autonomic center, adding brain cells by the millions to this important brain compartment.

To pay high tribute to yourself, to ennoble yourself, to lift yourself in your own estimation, you find your highest qualities. To dwell upon that which is favorable in your life, to elevate yourself in soul, to give yourself up to exalted self communion, to aspire to lofty positions, even in the imagination, improves, develops, ennobles, leads to self promotion without fail. It pays better dividends than stocks and bonds, besides it develops the soul and prepares you for eternity. It will make you honest in action, honorable in conduct and make you a better Christian.

A COMPARISON OF SELF EXALTATION AND SELF DEPRECIATION

The self-exalted man forgets his unfavorable past; the man who depreciates himself lives in the unfavorable acts of the past, and may commit shameful acts constantly. His life is a constant regret.

He condemns himself. How can he advance? Self exaltation lives a good life, thinks high thoughts, does noble deeds; self depreciation thinks bad thoughts, lives a bad life, does ignoble deeds. Self exaltation lives in the *Great Within* and becomes nobler; self depreciation lives in the lower self and becomes ignoble. Self exaltation attends to its own business; self depreciation is familiar and meddles with the business of others.

Self exaltation lifts people in their own eyes and finds their higher qualities; self depreciation finds their lowest qualities and tells them to others. Self exaltation has something good to say about all; self depreciation is often a scandal monger. Self exaltation is satisfied with the opinion of self; self depreciation knocks for praise at every door, however humble. Self exaltation governs and leads; self depreciation serves, learns, complains and grumbles.

Self exaltation is serene, strong, steady in nerves, high minded and elevates others to high positions; self depreciation is restless, unsteady, nervous, high tempered, often at war with self and others, common, envious and climbs up by pulling others down.

Self exaltation is exclusive and select; self depreciation is common, cheap and familiar. Self exaltation accomplishes more with less brain, effort, capital, training, education, opportunity; self depreciation accomplishes nothing only worries, complains and depends upon wages and job hunting. Self exaltation brings better children and trains them into noble, useful men and women; it builds a lasting character; eradicates idle weeds from brain and soul; uses energies for high purposes; builds brain; cultivates noble sentiments; makes every move count; and turns idle energies, waste, knowledge and powers into gold. It lifts other people to a higher level, inspires them to noble deeds, calls out latent power in self and others, thus becoming popular without trying. Self depreciation becomes unpopular even when trying to make self popular.

Sow self exaltation and you reap soul peace and personal influence. Sow self depreciation and temper and you reap thistles and enemies. Sow lust and you reap disease. Sow bashfulness and you reap servitude and failure. Feel great and you become greater. Feel important and you appear and act important. Delight in your own company and you become serene; and, will not crave cinemas to amuse you; excitement to thrill you; diamonds to ornate your fingers; dress to make you appear important at a time you know within yourself that you are not what you try to appear. Exalt yourself; exalt others. Lead others and yourself in a magnanimous manner.

Exaltation leads, wisdom knows, opposition and dogmatism argue, temper quarrels, vanity fears, bashfulness trembles, but self exaltation is always serene, dignified, reposeful. An exalted soul is always magnetic in the sense of being popular. An exalted personality attracts without trying, but discontent produces repulsion. Praise a man at the same time you look for, and discover, his faults for purposes of scandal, invite him to lunch and blow your own trumpet of self praise and vanity, and you cannot win his esteem. He may not know you as you are, but he feels his soul contract and darken in your presence! He feels little and cheap, and avoids you forever. This is not exalting, ennobling to you nor to him. Noble thoughts ennoble, exalted sentiments exalt, aspiring sentiments inspire, altruism rebuilds humanity, piety sanctifies the soul, faith in self leads to self action and enterprises.

Distrust or mistrust may also be called difference, being the opposite of self confidence. Bashfulness acts on the mind like choke-gas on breathing. Cynicism is often the offspring of self depreciation, or lack of faith in self, humanity, God and progress. Such negative qualities make enemies as fast as it rains in Scotland when the atmosphere is misty.

Cultivate faith in yourself, faith in the people, faith in the future, faith in nature, faith in the abstract, faith in God, faith in development, faith in the noble forces that run the universe, faith in your plans, faith in the hereafter and call this faith whatever you please.

Trust in statements, in divine testimonies, in religion and pecuniary worth, in moral probity and call it whatever you please. For it is not important what you call it; it is more important that you have it. Hope for that which you believe in, but do not hope for success and believe in failure. Do not hope for health and believe in disease. Do not hope to develop, yet believe that it cannot be done. If you lack faith, trust, confidence and hope, you are unbalanced and *must* build brain cells or go under.

When we lack self confidence, we feel bashful and get into a groove and stay there against will and interest. Then, we must build brain cells in the faculty of self liberation and self recognition. The cynic distrusts himself, his future, his God, all the people, government, the hereafter, health and everything else. His wings of faith do not carry him very high. Poor man! He is doomed because he is his own destiny maker, his own punishment, his own misery, his own failure and his own pain. He will not listen. Like a man who stands alongside a purse containing ten thousand dollars and stubbornly refuses to bend his stiff back to pick it up. He'll look, because he cannot believe, and he remains the same poor, miserable disbeliever and cynic. He must go his own miserable way, while we, who can believe, trust and hope become happy and prosperous, because we are our own destiny makers through brain building. We engineer ourselves, and by so doing, we also engineer our own destiny.

IS SELF EXALTATION SELF IDOLATRY AND SELF CONCEIT?

Many good Christians are afraid that self exaltation leads to self conceit, self righteousness, self idolatry, selfishness, insolence, self infatuation, self love and other ignoble qualities. But self exaltation leads to the very opposite—self ennoblement and piety. Such ignoble qualities spring from the lower man and are twin brothers to self contempt, self abuse, suicide, self torture, vanity, effrontery, etc. There is a heaven-wide difference between them and self exaltation. Self conceit boasts but self exaltation does not. Self conceit is haughty but self exaltation is civil, courteous and dignified. Self conceit finds others low, simple, crude and contemptible; self exaltation sees good qualities in all. Self conceit indulges in low deeds and misuses self and others; self exaltation ennobles self and others and never stoops to low deeds. Self conceit boasts until friend and foe are disgusted; self exaltation forgets self and edifies others.

One of my many trips brought me to India and Sai Babba. I learned a great deal from his teaching as well as from so many others. I remember a woman asked Sai Babba if he had noticed any difference in her since their last visit. He answered "no" to the woman. She said, "But I have tried so very hard throughout the years to make a difference." He answered her, "You don't understand, I found you perfect the first time I saw you."

Self conceit is bold, brazen, insolent, loutish, repulsive. Self conceit springs from the lower man; self exaltation comes from the higher man, and is God-like in nature. Self exaltation says that there is something divine and sacred in every man, while self conceit argues that all are rascals. Self conceit is overbearing and has no respect for anyone, not even for self.

The self-exalted man respects himself and others, and is thankful to God, parents and teachers for what he is.

He feels his own worth, guards himself, controls himself and acts like a true nobleman. We can never over exalt, over ennoble ourselves. But most of us under exalt, under estimate, dishonor, depreciate ourselves and do things that should be left undone.

If we truly believe we are created in the image of God, that we are God-like, we would feel, think, act and look differently. "Ye are Gods," said Christ. A God dwells in our *Great Within*, although we do not know it, feel it, act it, believe it, look it. We must learn to know what we are and what we should be.

MAN WHO CHANGED

Anyone who reads this course, if only once, will be a different man or woman, forever after. Anyone who applies this course for one year, or for life, will reorganize himself or herself, until either knows his or her high birth, great possibilities, important mission and noble origin. We are all sons and daughters of *The Most High*.

Lesson 8 reminds us of and reinforces the importance of the principle that we reap as we sow. Sowing is what we allow ourselves to think, feel and experience. If we want good fruit, we have to sow good seed.

Do you know why flowers grow? They grow to get out of the dirt!

LESSON 8

CARE IN WHAT YOU THINK,
HEAR, READ, EAT AND DRINK

We are what we sow in heart, brain and soul, nothing more, nothing less. We are what we think, feel, know, see, hear, read, eat, drink, breathe, do, dare, try and develop.

The thoughts you think, the sentiments you dwell on, the knowledge you gather, the friends you keep, and that which you see, hear, read, eat, drink, breathe, dare and do sum up what you are and what you will be. So be careful with whom you associate, what you think, feel, see, hear, read, eat, drink, breathe, try, dare, do and *how* you develop yourself.

HAVE ANYTHING—BUT YOU HAVE TO
HAVE ALL THAT GOES WITH IT

If you read the daily "scandal sheet," what will become of you? If you inhale smog air, smoke, gases, chemical fumes, etc., what will become of you? If you attend cinemas, shows, bars, race tracks, casinos, pool rooms and so on, will you develop your higher self? We may fool people and ourselves, but we cannot fool nature. Whatever we do for ourselves, we do for ourselves and *must* take the consequences. What is done is done.

FOOD FOR THE BRAIN AND NERVES

Well-beaten egg white with goat cream
Fish eggs, good ice cream with Swedish rye crisp
Clam broth and yellow corn bran broth combined
Fish eggs, cod roe, salmon eggs
Oyster broth, fish broths, veal joint broth
Steamed smelt, white fish, sardines
Fresh fish bone broths, barley, green kale soups
Milk, fresh, warm and foaming from the goat
Raw goat milk, goat cream and goat butter
Gelatins - fruit
Whole rice with rice polishings
Chlorella
Nut butters (almond, etc.), seed butters (sesame, etc.)
Colostrum, bee pollen
Egg yolk, fertile—from chickens that live on the ground.
Foods never fried or cooked in heat above 212 degrees F.
Berries, all black. Foods that have lots of seeds
Sprouts, lecithin, sunflower seeds, chia seeds
Black cherries, mulberries, raspberries
Dr. Jensen's Whole Life Food Blend
Bamboo shoots, okra, squash, cucumbers
Raw sugar cane
Original foods such as mung beans, alfalfa
Persimmons, pomegranates, quinces, figs, guava
Avoid seedless foods and hybrids.

The brain requires animal phosphorus, lecithin, albumin, sodium chloride, also other brain food elements.

MAN'S GREATEST HEALTH BUILDER

Without fear of contradiction, good blood, a constructive blood building diet, plenty of sleep before twelve at night and a cheerful disposition, are man's greatest health builders. The great questions are, what are good blood building foods? What is a constructive diet? My advice is to read my book,

Vibrant Health From Your Kitchen, which lists the Five Sins in Civilization.

DOES THE SOUL FEEL HEAT, COLD, PAIN?

Is the soul sensitive to heat, cold or pain? Our body is nothing but a lump of earthy matter and liquid. We are made of sixteen chemical elements. Drive the soul out of the body with an anesthetic, and the body is comparatively dead until the soul returns.

We can cut, slash, carve, burn, punch, saw as much as we please in nerve, bone and tissue, yet the anesthetized patient feels and knows no more than a corpse what is taking place in the old body. The nerves cannot feel, the eyes cannot see, the ears cannot hear, the brain cannot reason. After the soul shall have departed, the body can be frozen as stiff as an icicle in Siberia, or boiled for hours without knowing anything about the treatment. Surely it is not the body that is sensitive to the doctor's dope, the surgeon's knife, to Siberian frigidity, to pain, to rattlesnake poison, to torrid heat, to barometric humidity, to atmospheric pressure. It is the soul that feels through the nerves, but the nerves are dead. Feelings are in the soul.

PROTECTING YOUR HEAT CENTERS

Between the naval and the *pubis* are the plexuses that centralize in the chest brain. This part develops great heat in times of fever. Subsidiary heat centers are also found at the cervical region of the spine. Many people are sensitive to heat and cold between the *os pubis* and the *umbilicus*, also at the back of the neck, under the chin, at the lumbar sacral junction, at the ankles and wrists.

All ailing parts are sensitive to cold and heat and should be protected. The soul is the sufferer. All sorts of sensations center in the soul. Most diseases have their roots in the soul. We cannot cure the soul with poison or with the surgeon's knife.

We should protect our body, especially the heat centers and prevent painful sensations and diseases by correct eating.

DEVELOPING YOUR MOST POTENT POWER CENTER

Autonomy means that by building in new cells where this faculty has its seat, you will become your own law. Bashfulness vanishes, timidity disappears, stage fright will never bother, lack of self confidence will be a spook of the past, and fears will evanesce like a fog in the sun. You will be a new person. You will act and cause other people to act. No more nervousness, no confusion, no gloom. Nothing disturbs your serenity of mind. Convince yourself by saying to yourself many times a day: **Nothing can disturb me unless I give it my consent.**

Nothing disturbs me, nothing makes me restless. I am like a serene landscape. I am my own companion, the fullness of my life, my own master, my own leader. I depend upon no one for counsel, help, knowledge, money making. I enjoy my own sacred presence. I am self content, self pleased, and can decide puzzling questions. I am able to forget and go on in my own noble way without trouble. I do not worry; nothing makes me nervous; I have perfect control over my nerves. Ears, eyes, fingers, thoughts and senses obey me. I am master of myself.

I live in a high soul altitude. I am lofty, exalted, determined to live a noble life. I live in my *Great Within*, charged and recharged with a power that comes from the Most High, a power that nothing can resist, nothing can conquer, a might that prevails over weakness. I have wonderful power concealed within, a power that I shall use now and forever, a power that I feel within my inner being, a power that shall double and treble my efficiency, more and more as the wheels of time roll forward. I shall make suggestions to myself of my own great power within, until I am convinced that I am invincible, that I have conquered the lower man and all negative qualities, including bashfulness. I am mighty, independent, self acting, free. I feel myself grow in strength, patience, control, resignation. I can meet anything and win through firmness, self control, patience, self composure and tranquility.

I win without battle, prevail without arms, retrieve without force, convince without arguments, overcome without struggle, persuade without words, please without trying, act without opposition, remain serene in the midst of turmoil, commotion and quarrel. Why?

Because I live in my *Great Within*, in my greatest power center, where a current of power streams in from the Great Master Builder of the universe. I am in contact with my God, and can win without powder and artillery. I feel my power, my own greatness because I am in contact with the Master of all Masters, the one who lives within my *Great Within*, with the Almighty that holds the sun in its course and the planets in their orbits through His power. I am one with Him and He is one with me. What do I care for praise, flattery, blame and criticism? The bullets of blame fall harmless at my feet. Noble hearted, I move forward like a noble steed. The arrows of defamation cannot reach me, for I soar in soul far beyond their height or range.

My reputation is beyond reproach. I am the same exalted person whatever the people say against me or in favor of me. I have found my higher self and can say as Paul said, "None of these things move me." Wonderful are my possibilities, for I am made in the image of God, born to command, sway and subdue, not by force of arms or arguments, but peacefully. I have God in my very being, endlessness in my *Great Within*, eternity reflects itself in my soul, and I am drawn nearer to nature and to nature's God.

I feel my *Great Within* expand with power and might. I stand like a statue of repose in time of commotion. I am like a human oak of strength, able to prevail against devastating storms and hurricanes. I feel that self exaltation brings me nobility and soul peace. I live in my exalted self hood, in the *Great Within*, in lofty aspirations for high attainments, noble purposes, exalted aims, in elevated sentiments. I can master myself, my thoughts and my habits. I have a sacred personality, an imposing influence and a power to prevail against evil forces. I am punctual, orderly, systematic, able to concentrate my thoughts, focus my mind on any sentiment that I please. I have myself under perfect control.

My greatness needs no superficial props, such as money, beauty, praise, titles, finery, dress, luxury, wealth, education, advantages. The greatness is in **myself**, in **my** *Great Within*.

If you make such suggestions to yourself daily, hourly; if you talk, reason, think, muse and dwell on your own greatness and live within your higher self—you are building brain cells in your most potent power center. The soul has only *one* faculty that is the commander-in-chief of mind, body and emotions. You are developing this very faculty of power.

The following chapter is a lesson on mastery that you will never forget. If you can master yourself, you can master anything else.

FROM THE HEART TO THE WORLD

If there be righteousness in the heart
There will be beauty in the character.

If there be beauty in the character
There will be harmony in the home.

If there be harmony in the home
There will be order in the nation.

If there is order in the nation
There will be peace in the world.

-Confucius

LESSON 9

YOU, THE MASTER
OF YOUR OWN DESTINY

Left to ourselves, we think that destiny cannot be
mastered; that fate cannot be controlled; that lot cannot be
directed; that doom cannot be prevented. People think that
destiny is marked out; fate is fixed; lot assigned; doom passed;
that we have no preventive power over either. This is true so
long as we permit ourselves to drift and be governed by the
lower man. But when we take ourselves in charge, lastly we
become masters of our own destiny, fate, lot and prevent doom
from being passed over our heads for our own bad conduct.

One man is lucky; another is unlucky; one man succeeds;
the other fails; one man goes free; the other is jailed or hanged.
We claim that we have a great will; that we are free agents;
that we can act or not act. Do we not have a free will? You
would say yes. Destiny, lot, fate and doom depend upon *how*
we use our will, freedom, mind, emotions, thoughts; how we
talk and act; where we live; what we eat and drink; what we
study, see, hear and read; how we scatter our forces and drift;
and how we engineer ourselves.

Every word we utter; every thought we think; every
sentiment we dwell upon; every emotion that agitates the brain
cells, every impulse, fear, passion, plan, argument, motion,
feeling, wish or act uses up nerve force and vitality. That little
member, the tongue, has caused more trouble and killed more
people than all the wars; more people than the doctor's dope
and poisons have killed since the days of Hippocrates. We
become vitality wasters. Fatigue syndrome develops. The host
dies out and is depreciated as all types of disease walk in. To
control the tongue is to control the mind, to live long and

remain healthy. Most of us need a tongue vacation, a nerve rest, a liberal brain diet, though we may not know it nor believe it. Take out emergency time for yourself.

No man has more influence than the silent, conservative, exalted, watchful listener. He listens to this man, to the reasons of that man, to the plans of the third man, to the discussion of a fourth, to the consultation of a whole assembly of men. He listens, watches says nothing but looks wise. He arouses the curiosity of all. At last, when he does talk, he is prepared. He has listened to the plans and advice of all the experts, and knows what they know and more than he knew when he entered. He is a reservation man. He wins because of silence, tongue control, self mastery, nerve vitality, influence and mind control. Others marvel at his genius, prudence and wisdom. He masters his own destiny and even that of others.

PILOT MAKING GOOD TIME BUT LOST

Here is a good lesson for the wisest of you. Wait for *your* opportunity. It is coming! But then you should be prepared. Listen and say nothing. Be wise in silence. Save your nerve force until it is needed. We are always repairing and not doing enough preparing. Talk when it pays. Keep your affairs, thoughts and plans to yourself. Dwell on sentiments, of self exaltation. People talk themselves into trouble, litigation, failure and disease. The tongue, in many, is on a pivot, as busy as a needle in a sewing machine. They talk, fuss, worry, rush, tear, jerk, jump, scold, scream, argue early and late and wear out the patience of people, lose their children's respect, their own fortitude and the toleration of visitors. Their health fails; they suffer from nervousness, dyspepsia, sleeplessness, liver ailments and nervous prostration. They call in their learned doctors who do not understand the cause of the trouble and are given morphine for sleeplessness, hydrastis for liver complaints, arsenic for neurasthenia, *nux vomica* for dyspepsia, and their pocketbook is gradually cured, but the trouble goes on. They try different climates, mud baths, vacations, and all cures under the sun.

At this point, we want to go over how we take care of our patients and how we take care of disease. The host attracts the disease. We take care of the patient and not the disease. Otherwise we are taking care of symptoms and not the disease.

Self mastership, or a course in self culture, would stop their mental machinery; close their mouths; give their tongues a vacation; keep their emotions quiescent; save their nerve force; their pocketbooks; their own life; their children's love; honor and respect; a kind of doctoring that doctors have not yet studied; namely, a grain of common sense.

Learn to bridle your tongue; practice silence. If people abuse you, say nothing, but look wise. If they urge your opinion, tell them that the matter has many sides. If they ask you familiar questions, change the subject tactfully and politely. If they want you to interfere, give them to understand that you prefer to run your own business and not meddle with the business of other people. Intelligence cannot argue with an uneducated man. Thus, you become master of the situation. You conserve your brain force; you win respect; you become distinguished; and the engineer of your own destiny, because you avoid trouble by your prudent policy.

WINNING PUBLIC CONFIDENCE

There is something imposing, attractive, lofty, reposeful about the leader. His walk, voice, manners, personality, deportment, appearance fill us with respect and confidence. We feel that we can repose trust in him without titles and recommendations. One glance at him and we are one. People of affairs come to him. Leadership is its own reward; its own recommendation. The leader is given positions of trust without self solicitation. *That which we admire, those that we imitate, that which we long and wish for—we become.*

BOX OF BIRDS—SEVEN MILES OF BAD ROAD

You cannot aspire for leadership; you cannot fill yourself with exalted sentiments daily; you cannot imitate the leader in voice, walk, action and manners; you cannot clinch your fists, tense your muscles, fill your lungs with air; you cannot assume one single attitude given in this course; you cannot dwell on one single thought; you cannot stand still and look wise; you cannot feel great and lofty; you cannot stand erect, slightly curved backwardly above the breastbone; you cannot carry a full chest whether full of air or not; you cannot draw in your chin; you cannot widen your nostrils by deep breaths; you cannot look into the distant space about one foot above your nearest man; you cannot observe everything coldly, outwardly; nor carry yourself with an air of superiority; you cannot move forward and walk as if you were walking on steel springs, on the balls of the feet, without swinging your shoulders or being behind or ahead of your feet with your body, without swinging, swaying, rocking movements of your body as you walk, and swinging your arms below the elbows only, holding your stomach and pressing your chest, as you move forward say three hundred steps, at the same time as you feel as noble and imperious as an exalted lord—you cannot do all this in private without changing your appearance, influence, talent, disposition or your very brain and soul. Do this a few months, and your friends will say, what are you doing with yourself—you look and act and speak so differently!

People will act as I have seen them act in New Zealand. When you meet someone and ask, "How are you today?" They will say, "I feel like a box of birds." What a challenging moment for you to look toward the lighter things! Then when another person is met on the road, they say, "You look like seven miles of bad road this morning." You will find that an inner thing begins to develop. You begin to supply other people with a feeling that they feel differently when they meet you. You give out an expression. "It has been said ... that he had a countenance that outshone the sun." How would you like to have that come out of you? That is why I believe we live on what we pour out. The inner self will be so different that it will be difficult for others to measure. It will be like, at one time, I

69

had someone taking our class and when they were about to go home, he said, "You know I feel so different. I feel so much better. I feel like walking on air." I got a card from him a week later and he said, "When I got home, I had changed so much for the better that my own dog didn't know me, and he bit me."

All people will notice the difference. It is not necessary to tell them what you are doing. They need not know. Your training is a sacred, exclusive, exalted drill in self mastery, personality, leadership, serenity, self recognition, self command, public recognition and unfolding of the *Great Within*.

GOVERN THROUGH YOUR EYES

Behind your eyes is your wonderful, immortal soul, a heavenly dynamo of tremendous energy. The brain is the soul's workshop. Thus the eyes are great, potent centers of energy. Love, sympathy, devotion, influence and will center in the eyes. Intellectual, magnetic, volatile and emotive energy acts through the eyes, providing the mind acts in a concentrative and prolonged manner. But a drifting mind cannot use its power however great the power may be. Hypnotists, ferocious beasts, black magicians, venomous serpents, mad dogs, dishonorable plotters, insolent despots, intrepid generals, oily confidence men may often become so completely intimidated that further progress may be impossible, under the influence of the mere still gaze of a master mind. It is important that you (or anyone of us) learn to use the eyes steadily, ceaselessly, concentrating — not by fits, starts and periods, but ceaselessly. Learn to dwell with your mind on the question (sale, purchase, plan, etc.), and keep your eyes on the person without winking or removal of mind and eyes until the matter is settled, and you are using your mind, brain and eyes or at least you are learning to do so. Your eyes are more powerful than your fists, gun, voice, tongue or pen. You cannot conquer your foe by killing, him; besides killing, it is mean, ugly, criminal and cowardly. Win him by your eyes; ennoble him; let him improve himself;

ennoble himself; work for you or in your interest; and, he will bless you now and in eternity.

If we cannot do good, we should at least not do evil, if we are noble and exalted. Use your eyes not your fist; your brain not your gun; your reason not a stick; leadership not poison; common sense not hypnotism; magnanimity not flattery.

Make a friend of your enemy and ennoble him. This is real Christianity. Center your mind, your will, your purpose in your eye, and do the same with your eyes as the photographic lens does—*focus* and never cease until you win.

It is more important that you conquer yourself, govern yourself, regulate, systematize, lead, ennoble and develop yourself, than it is to conquer, handle and lead others. To win, we must focus eyes; dwell with mind and thought; center energy; concentrate on plans and purposes; steadily and ceaselessly until we win.

Loud talk, hard fists, fuss, rush, words, bluster, boisterous oratory, eagerness, fear or foolish actions never win in love, business or professions nor in any kind of training. Use brain, eyes, reason, will and self exaltation ceaselessly; and learn to focus mind and thought without cessation, and you win. Your eyes are power centers. Do not pour out your oratory and pound with your fists in the air or on tables. Do not jump like a gorilla on public platforms; do not grin like a monkey; sneer like a cynic; laugh and talk like a clown; giggle like a young girl; glare like a rattler; shrug your shoulders and wink; play with people or make sport of them, but feel, think, look and learn to master eye, fingers, feet, thoughts, senses, gestures, actions and emotions.

Learn to look consciously and ceaselessly at some distant object without winking for one to three minutes. That object may be the eye of a friend, a finger, a post, a glass, etc. It is immaterial what you look at, just so you practice without cessation when you practice. It is *the practice, the application,* that does the work.

In Lesson 10, look forward to learning the do's and don't's, common-sense steps to self exaltation. You'll never be the same after reading it.

LESSON 10

WHAT YOU SHOULD AND SHOULD NOT DO

Never talk in a loud voice, but always gently.
Never tell ugly, unbelievable stories.
Never go to excess in anything.
Avoid questionable associates.
Establish a reputation for honesty and punctuality.
Give your blood freedom to flow unimpeded by corsets,
belts, etc.
Keep your own knowledge to yourself until you can use it.
Cultivate courage, but be like an oiled bullet—silent.
Never be noisy.
Guard your character; it is your highest attainment.
Use tact in public by dwelling upon exalted sentiments.
Cultivate cheerfulness of mind.
Keep your own trouble and pains to yourself.
Always be civil, courteous, polite.
Look for good points in people.
Look for your own good points.
Let no one force you, and do not fight nor argue.
Let no one rule; act and be silent.
Do not read newspapers, nor anything of a low nature.
Live much in seclusion and select noble friends.
Avoid promiscuous sex commerce; it is degrading.
Listen to *how* people speak. Notice how they look, act,
what they talk about. Watch their faces when you talk to them
and you know *how* it affects them.

HOW TO CARRY YOURSELF

Carry yourself uprightly and stately, with the center of gravity on the balls of your feet. The gravity of your body should follow your advanced foot when you walk. Stately positions are supported on a single base. Do not walk on your heels tramp the floor, hold your feet apart when you stand, rock up and down on your toes, swing to and fro. Keep yourself poised. Stand still on the public platform and do not jump about like a pugilist nor rant like an evangelist. Stand on a narrow base and control your voice and gestures.

Feel self exalted and you will be poised and self composed; your attitude will be imposing, and you will look like a man, even a nobleman. Walk with a full chest, an erect head, a stately bearing, neither leaning forward, backward, nor sideways. Let your hands hang at your side. Feel self exalted and you do not need books, courses and teachers to train you. Self exaltation does more for grace, deportment, manners and appearance than books and teachers. We should feel right before we look noble and cultured. Culture is in the man not in books, teachers and universities.

THE COMMON MAN, THE MANLY MAN
AND THE NOBLEMAN

There is a great difference between the common man, the manly man, and the nobleman. We must not be common so long as we build brain cells in the autonomic center in the brain. If we feel that we can sit with anyone, walk with anyone, go to church with anyone, talk with anyone, visit anyone, call on anyone, go to any kind of places, join any kind of club, read any trash, daily papers, novels, or act, speak, think in any way that the Old Adam dictates, yet be just as good as any one, we are already merely common men and women.

If we read the daily papers, we are common. If we use slang and bow to public opinion, we are common. If we dress in a disgraceful manner because it is stylish, we are common. If we are base or low minded, or if we prostitute our person, principles or knowledge, we are common. If we gossip, swear, lie, steal, practice trickery, fool people, tease children, torment animals, we are very common, indeed.

If we fight or approve of low sport, we are common. If the autonomy center in the brain is below par, we are common in each case. If we are familiar, we are common. If we are pleasure loving, we are common. If we are proud and haughty, we are common. If we are common, we are not exalted, exclusive, noble, select. We should not be "as good as anyone"; we should be equal to the best, if not *the best*, but we should not think about it, nor talk about it to others, nor compare ourselves to others in the sense of being superior, for this is self conceit.

Our superiority should not be compared superiority, but unconscious superiority, or a godlike sentiment of self exaltation and a holy desire to ennoble all people, ourselves included, and raise self and others to a higher altitude. What is a man? What is a woman? A man who is a *real* man or a woman who is a *real* woman, has those masculine or feminine qualities that are peculiar to a manly man or to a womanly woman. In a manly man, these qualities are:

Stability	Resolution
Muscularity	Gallantry
Bone compactness	Courage
Character	Working energy
Honor	Principle
Probity	Self confidence
Fortitude	Industriousness
Insight	Inflexibility of purpose
Moneymaking capacity	

Such a man cares but little for society life, popularity, style and modernism. He is a manly man and not a common man.

A womanly woman has feminine qualities, namely:

Virtue	Sense of decency
Chastity	Love of beauty
Neatness	Love of home
Modesty	Love of children
Affection	Sociability
Devotion	Neighborliness
Sympathy	Service
Morality	Femininity

Such a woman is a wifely wife, a good mother, perfect housekeeper, a good neighbor. She is not common in mind and disposition.

A nobleman is a nobleman by nature, self training, self culture, not by titles, wealth, station, advantages, heritage and the like. He is moved by the higher faculties. Such a man is self exalted, self acting, self dependent, noble, serene, self composed, honest, punctual, a natural-born leader of self or others or of national or international affairs. He lifts us to a higher level. He is a manly man who has made a nobleman of himself by living in his *Great Within.*

THE KEY TO SUCCESS AND PROMOTION

Self recognition demands exclusiveness and personal reserve. That which is rare, select, sacred, exclusive, esoteric, we value more than that which is common. Self association, self communion, self exaltation lead to greater self recognition and self poise.

This course is for the one interested in driving for higher endeavors. Your books, course, things, knowledge must be as select or sacred as you are exclusive. Your opinion is not a common opinion for everybody. Keep it to yourself. It is gold, not common beef-wit.

You should not talk much with people, associate with them, make yourself common. Be unreachable, select, exclusive, sacred, seldom seen nor heard, except on the public platform or on special occasions. You never saw God, did you?

Do you know why? When you are through with your speech, you should disappear.

This course is for the one interested in driving for the higher endeavors in life. Truly we will be measured by our endeavors.

The more you associate with yourself, the more you commune with yourself, and the less you are seen in ordinary life, the more exclusive you become; the more you exalt yourself and the more you know and see of yourself, the more you honor yourself; the more earnestly you search for your great qualities—to that same extent you will win. You develop the spirit of self recognition. You will go to yourself for knowledge, advice, guidance, information, aid, work, service, patronage, reasons, amusements, honor, joy, pleasure, rest, recreation, enterprise, decision. This develops you, and you become greater and greater. Here, as elsewhere, self exaltation is the secret of all, self recognition included.

Sociability cannot be developed by going to dances, by talking, laughing, visiting, inviting people to feasts, banquets and dinners. This has nothing to do with sociability nor with social, personal attraction. To develop sociability, the social brain or soul qualities should be cultivated. In proportion as the social brain is developed, in the same proportion will peace reign in the soul.

A sociable person is at peace with himself, with family, neighbors, relations, friends, churches, unions, clubs, societies, governments, foreigners and other nations, also with the whole creation and with his God. Peacefulness, unity, neighborliness, kindness, love, sympathy, amity, brotherhood, fidelity, mutuality, faith in humanity, trust, association and a sociable nature go hand in hand. If all people had normal, sociable qualities, there would never be war, struggle, quarrel, divorce, strife, enmity and contention.

DEVELOPING SOCIABILITY

To cultivate sociability, it is not necessary to mingle with people. You can cultivate sociable qualities by yourself. Here is the secret:

1. Think kindly of men, women and children.

2. Find their good qualities and never their unfavorable qualities.
3. Feel that they are your friends and that you are their friend.
4. Give a good interpretation to their every act, expression and motive.
5. Think much of their good qualities.
6. Be civil to all.
7. Please them and agree with them, but lead, nevertheless.
8. Treat animals kindly and handle tender plants gently.

Do this daily and think of it hourly and you will develop those peace-bringing, loving, gentle and sociable qualities. To mingle with people, talk, argue, find fault, think ill of this one and take a dislike to that one, is a good way to freeze out the sociable qualities. Late hours are bad for the nerves, also for the social brain. All nature is wrapped in serene slumber the first half of the night. Flowers and buds close their little "eyes" as night approaches. All nature is negative, still and serene at this time. This is the restful period for the nervous system and the social brain. Sleep at this time rests the brain cells; soothes the nerves; refreshes the mind; tranquilizes the soul; generates nerve force; increases social influence; and gives nature an opportunity to carry away fatigue products. It is called the magnetic rest period. If you feel and think that people are your friends and you are their friend, and if you always try to find their good qualities, you are developing the social brain.

Most of the true secrets of great leadership have been hidden in the past. If you are ready to learn them, many good and wise pointers await you in Lesson 11.

Great Spirits have always encountered violent opposition from mediocre minds.

-ALBERT EINSTEIN

LESSON 11

ARE YOU NERVOUS?

If you are nervous, intense, impetuous, high tempered and moved by stormy emotions and wild impulses, you need neuro-static exercises, sociable, even-minded companions, protein foods, slightly prolonged breathing exercises, brain and nerve foods, rest, sleep in abundance, recreation, salty sponge baths, a fairly moist climate, under the influence of self exaltation. Nervousness is unknown to people who are led by the faculty of autonomia, the self-leadership faculty. It is the coolest faculty of the mind.

A great many noble people often wonder how to win public recognition through cultured self management in public spheres. Here we have the secret, which is really nothing but common sense:

Lead the conversation to noble topics.
Watch your every act.
Listen. Set other people talking.
Watch others.
Be still.
Fill your mind with exalted sentiments.
Speak in low, distinct, conversational tone of voice.
Act with deliberation, if you act at all.
Be civil, complaisant, deferent, courteous.
Be gallant to women, polite to professionals, kind to
  children, humane to all, and kind to animals.
Build self exaltation.
Have consideration for the rights of others.
Practice personal stillness.
Be prompt in action.

Be deliberate in speech.
Recognize the customs of society.
Observe silence when possible and appropriate.
Pay attention.
Practice unobserved watchfulness.

These are nearly all the essentials for public recognition and self management in public spheres. Feel self exalted, and you are never at a disadvantage, never awkward, never disturbed, but always at ease among people, be they queens, kings, lords, nobles, plenipotentiaries, ministers, dudes, vain girls, society women or anyone else.

HOW SELF ASSOCIATION AND SELF COMMUNION TRAIN MINDS AND EDIFY SOULS

Sit down in the stillness of the evening and associate with yourself, being sure to enjoy your own companionship. Commune with your higher self, as you meditate and reason out your own greatness, dwelling on noble sentiments, living in your higher self, thinking of your own possibilities and your own sacred personality. Tell yourself that you are improving. Promise yourself prosperity and future happiness. Cultivate sentiments of joy and hope.

Find peace and serenity in your own company. Be your own companion. Become pleased with yourself and content whatever your lot may be. Let the past die and live for the future. Make noble resolutions and be true to your resolutions. Sit down every evening in your own sacred presence and commune with yourself for fifteen minutes to one hour before you retire, thinking of your own greatness, advantages, noble acts, important knowledge, sacred personality, power of control, health, progress, high qualities, self composure, influence, etc., until you *know* and *feel* within yourself that *your are* what you think and say you are.

This leads to self recognition, self action, serenity of mind, nerve calm, soul peace and self contentment. It expands your soul, widens the horizon of your mind, gives you a different appearance, leads to nobler acts. You will speak in a different tone of voice, for it gives scope to your voice, reach to your mind, altitude to your aspirations, self hood to your personality or what people call influence, address, attraction and personality. Self exaltation develops all of those qualities, but self exaltation demands privacy, exclusiveness, self association, self communion and self nobility.

That which people call personality can be included under the word self exaltation. Your appearance, deeds, great plans, high purposes, noble aims, sublime aspirations, address, self control, tone of voice, stillness, focused eyes, close attention, nerve control, bodily control, tongue control, use of knowledge, dignity, cleanliness, courage, control of action, self distinction, tact, knowledge of human nature, stately carriage, full chest, dignified walk, steady eye, civility, reserve, attention to detail, watchfulness, pleasing manners and disposition to find the best qualities in yourself and in others—all the foregoing can be included under the word: personality; and self exaltation is the key to all. A self-exalted man is his own teacher. He acts the nobleman and has what people call personality. Why? Because all of his faculties act in unity because he is under the influence of self exaltation. This is, he is governed by the soul's commander-in-chief, namely the faculty which we call autonomia. He is building brain cells in that very faculty and becomes more and more self exalted, noble and influential. He develops all such admirable qualities. He is cool in the midst of turmoil.

Noble emotions give depth and range to breathing. Happiness, joy, love, increase respiration and lift the mind to higher altitudes. Happy, content, trustful, noble and exalted men and women live above their surroundings in a higher, nobler atmosphere, in their *Great Within*. They associate and commune with themselves. This is what you should do.

ACTING THE NOBLEMAN

When you act the nobleman, you hide your feelings. Your temper is foreign to you. Your face is like marble and no one knows what is going on in your mind. Your likes, dislikes, tendencies, impulses and opinions are known to yourself only,

You reveal nothing about yourself. You never talk about yourself. No one knows what you ate for breakfast; where you studied; how much you are worth; what you like or dislike; what your religion, politics, views, habits and hobbies are; what you intend to do; what you know and what you do not know.

You act behind a screen, hidden away from the world, yet popular and known near and far, but not privately known. No one can measure you, for you are too deep. You are never bothered or worried, but always composed. You never talk much, pay attention to trivia; you are never at a disadvantage, familiar, in a rush, or surprised. If someone shows you contempt, you say nothing, only look wise and lofty. You walk with your feet, not with your arms, head and body. Your eyes are still and penetrating. You see without looking, know without seeing, for you watch unobserved.

There is something unusual about you. You are like a statue of repose. If you were confronted with the gun of a desperado, you would not flinch. You look like a man of distinction. You are master of self and others. You can focus your whole mind on any question, plan, thought or sentiment. When people appeal to you, your sympathy is their sympathy. If they ask you for information, you are an information bureau. You are whole hearted. You never listen by halves. You are attention itself. Your mind acts in unity and is not like a circus of changes. Your thoughts are centered and are not on daily excursions. Neither do your emotions feed on stories, nor do you live in the daily papers. You act the nobleman because you are self exalted in mind and emotions. You are lifted in soul to higher heights.

HOW TO BECOME HAPPY AND REMAIN SO

He who searches for happiness outside of himself will be disappointed. He who searches for happiness within himself will *never* be disappointed. He who lives in his *Great Within*, in his highest, noblest sentiments finds happiness that endures. That happiness, which is born of money, possession, station, dress, luxury, idle pleasures, learning, titles, and the like, will dissipate like smoke. Self ennoblement and cell building in the higher, nobler faculty centers, through processes of cell building, produce an inborn or self-created happiness as eternal and firm as Gibraltar. The nobler your character, the happier your life. The exalted man lives his morals and lifts himself and others to higher levels and nobler deeds.

SELF ENNOBLEMENT

Self ennoblement comprises everything that relates to self improvement, or cell building in the highest, noblest soul centers of the brain. Health culture, sanitation, salubrious environments, climate, favorable bathing, intellectual training, religious culture, spiritual development, rest, recreation, cleanliness, nerve training, cultivation of the chest, training of the senses, fingers and muscles, normal evolution, wisdom rules, work that favors health, prose and humanity, can all be included under the word "self ennoblement." Self exaltation is the main key to all development, all culture. It leads to exclusiveness. Culture demands privacy. You should practice in private. Do not tell others anything about yourself, not even your wife, husband, mother, brother or sister. If you show this course to anyone, or reveal anything about yourself, you have already violated personal ethics, private rights and the laws of self culture. You have made yourself cheap and common. The common man or woman borrows from others, tells others of his wants, wishes, thoughts, studies, plans, intentions and belongings. Can he develop? He violates his own sacred personality and personal ethics every hour of the day. He has failed to understand what self exaltation is and has failed to apply it. Self ennoblement demands exclusiveness, a keen sense of self hood, a sense of our own sacred personality, sense of conviction of our own high origin.

SELF EVOLUTION AND PUBLIC RECOGNITION

It is not generally known that the soul has many functions and that the brain is the workshop of the soul. People admit that the intellect (the thinker) is located in the frontal lobe, and claim that love dwells in the heart. But when it is a question of will, judgement, appetite, attention, passion, nobility, honesty, honor, courage, invention, virtue, charity, hope and other characteristics—no psychologist, no scientist, no theologian, has yet discovered the seat of any one of such characteristics. Nor does anyone know that different thoughts, sentiments, memories, emotions, spring from different soul faculties and that a special kind of thought, emotion or desire develops a special faculty of center in the brain by the process of cell building (mitosis).

Here is the key to self development. Spiritual sentiments develop the spiritual faculty. Inventive thoughts develop the inventive faculty. Love develops love. Self exaltation develops the faculty of autonomia. This leads to self association, self recognition, self nobility, altruism, self mastery, influence, self evolution, public recognition and to high, exalted positions. Who would exalt a tramp to the throne? Look at the tramp and hear him babble, and would you not know that a tramp is a tramp, and that he could not govern a nation?

But when you find a self exalted, exclusive, masterly, select, reposeful, high-minded, imposing, controlled, just, noble, polite, spiritual, practical, self-possessed man, possessing all the qualities of leadership, he wins your esteem and you are willing to exalt him to high positions of trust. Thus self exaltation, self ennoblement, self evolution lead to public recognition.

Lesson 12 is one of the great keys to self exaltation. Self control and self mastery cannot be separated from self exaltation. Pay close attention to each of the following exercises.

LESSON 12

NOETIC EXERCISES AND ATTITUDES

Noetic exercises are more than physical culture exercises. They are mind, nerve and muscle exercises combined. They reach the nerves, the brain cells and the very soul.

BREATHING AFTER MEALS—EXERCISE 1

Always breathe deeply after meals. Take a little walk after each meal and breathe deeply from one hundred to two hundred breaths to favor digestion, oxidation and assimilation, being sure to call up exalted sentiments during such pleasure walks after eating.

STILL LIFE EXERCISES—EXERCISE 2

Feel exalted, great, noble. Fix your eyes and mind on your own eyes in a mirror. Take a long, full breath and hold it a few seconds; exhale all the air in the lungs without the slightest movement of the body, holding your chest immovable and shoulders down as you exhale. Inhale a long breath and repeat, standing as still as a statue for ten seconds at first, to forty seconds at last, after about six to ten months' practice. This exercise trains nerves and mind to stillness. Take this exercise over and over again.

RELAXATION PRACTICE—EXERCISE 3

Fill your mind with exalted sentiments, thinking of your great qualities and important mission in life. Sit still for five minutes in that same frame of mind until you feel exalted, controlled and noble. Now, as you sit in an upright position like a statue, filled with exalted sentiments, point at some object, figure on the wall or something else, keeping your mind and eyes on that figure so consciously that you see, hear or know of nothing else. Look at this figure one minute and not more than two minutes at first, without winking, breathing easily and naturally, but not forcefully. Now close your eyes and center your mind on your breath as it moves up and down in your chest, breathing naturally without any effort of will. Sit and breathe for ten to thirty minutes.

If you become relaxed to the point of sleepiness, retire for the night. If you do not become sleepy, keep your mind still on your breath as you dwell upon your greatness at the same time; then by an effort of your will, send your blood or a nerve wave or an exalted will impulse to the posterior crown of your head where the head begins to slope off to form the posterior crown.

This exercise relaxes you and attracts blood and nerve force to the autonomic brain area where the spirit of self exaltation dwells. It is a relaxing and cell-building exercise (neurostatic). Notice how calm, still, serene, peaceful you feel after taking this exercise.

You can originate still-life exercises yourself. *Still life wins.* When others are like boiling pots, you can stand before them like an oak of strength, wise and silent. Excitement, agitation, anxiety, worry, anger, rocking, swinging, drumming on tables, rocking on the heels and toes, swinging of the legs, stammering, crying, loud calling, winking, sighing, gaping, shaking the head, shrugging the shoulders, jumping, stuttering, sudden turns, bustle, radio noise, telephone rattle, wind, din, rattle, bluster, fuss, creeping, leaping and sudden stops all dissipate brain power, scatter nerve force, making us as restless as wildcats, as nervous as rabbits, as uneasy as monkeys. Let still life prevail in your *Great Within* at least thirty minutes a day to help you overcome the effects of nerve-racking habits cultivated early and late, Sunday and Monday, twelve hours a day or more.

SELF EXALTING ATTITUDE— DEVELOPING PERSONALITY—EXERCISE 4

Assume an exalted attitude. Stand erect, chin in, full immovable chest, considering yourself a nature's nobleman, as endless as space and time, as high in soul as the heaven above, high minded, heaven bred, solemn, noble, distant, exclusive, eminent, supreme, part of the great universe, and feeling as though a universe is coiled up in your soul.

Now fill your chest with air and employ the diaphragmatic method of breathing, in which your breath moves up and down in your chest without expansion and contraction of chest and without sideway, backward and forward chest movements. Now begin to move forward as a mighty potentate from two hundred to five hundred steps, assuming the same attitude as you walk, without moving the shoulders, walking with springy, lordly steps, without moving the upper arms or the upper body, only the lower arms below the elbows, looking in the distant space as you walk. Try this attitude as often as you can. It is the exalted attitude, noble gait, stately deportment of the nobleman or of the noble queen. A good idea is to write down on a black board *how* you should feel and think as you practice, for then you have it all before mind and eyes. Your mind is not yet accustomed to dwell long and consecutively on thoughts, sentiments, attitudes, breathing.

THE EXALTED TONE OF VOICE—EXERCISE 5

The exalted voice is low, distinct, steady, slightly metallic, authoritative, yet civil. Listen to a nobleman when he talks and imitate him. If you cannot find one, practice by yourself. Feel important, noble, great, exalted; carry a full chest; look steadily without winking; hold your head high; stand erect and as immovable as a statue. Advance with the right foot and stand

on the ball of this foot; point with the index finger of your right
hand and say in the same low, solemn, distinct, steady,
metallic, authoritative and civil voice: "I shall and will perform
my important mission in life nobly, for I feel that I am heaven
bred and sacred, that the Most High sent me here as a celestial
potentate to carry out this mission. All obstacles I shall and will
sweep aside nobly and serenely. I can die in the attempt, but
fail, *never!*"

All this is practice. Assume this attitude often, at a
specified time, for you should systematize your work, sleep,
meals, visits, studies, exercises from this on.

VOICE PRACTICE AND CULTURE—EXERCISE 6

Pay close attention to and listen to your own voice, when
your mind is exalted, chest tense, filled with air, when you are
peaceful, serene, fully conscious, looking into space above the
heads of people, or when you assume that same high minded
attitude previously mentioned; now speak in a clear, low,
steady voice as follows: "I am now listening to my own voice,
utterance, stress, accent, emphasis, for the purpose of judging
its vocal qualities, with the firm determination to improve my
voice, manners, attitude. I feel noble and exalted. Does my
voice do justice to my exalted personality?" As you speak,
stand before a mirror and study your manners, attitude,
appearance and be your own judge and teacher.

OVERCOMING TIMIDITY AND BASHFULNESS—
EXERCISE 7

Sit uprightly without resting against the chair; pay attention
to your breath as it moves up and down in your chest; fill your
soul with noble, exalted sentiments; dwell upon your greatness
and upon your moving breath at the same time. Close your eyes
and sit in this position ten to twenty minutes, measuring the
time to the second, if possible, without any conscious effort, or

looking at the clock; when the time is up inhale and exhale eight times.

Now look far beyond in space, eyes focused and point with your index finger to some hill, tree or mountain far beyond, as you dwell with your thoughts on your *Great Within* and speak as follows: "I am my own castle, my own strength, my own hope, my own master, leader, teacher, law, my own university. My own *Great Within* is my fort, my soul's sanctuary in which my God dwells. I live in Him and He dwells in me. He is exalted, sacred, great; *I* am exalted by emulation. I am *His* likeness, heaven bred, made in *His* image, fearfully and wonderfully made."

Sit in this position and speak so that you hear your own voice. Now lower your right hand and index finger and raise both hands as high as your shoulders to a distance of one foot from your eyes; hold your fingers limp and hanging down, as you still feel exalted; now tense your arms, neck, shoulders, but not your fingers, and send a nerve wave or blood current to the posterior crown of your head, thirty seconds, working up to one minute over a period of four months. Take this exercise every other day at specified times, always without fail.

Be true to yourself, to the course, to God, to your own rules or you are no nobleman, nor do you deserve success, prominence and exalted positions. It is a long and complex exercise, for you are forced to focus your mind simultaneously on several operations. This exercise does the work, arouses sleeping brain cells and builds new brain cells in the autonomy area of the brain.

HOW TO ADDRESS, INFLUENCE AND INTERVIEW PEOPLE—EXERCISE 8

In accosting, addressing, influencing or interviewing people, you should be at your best. Fill your mind with noble thoughts, exalted sentiments, convinced that your purpose is a noble one, that you are eager to lift people to a higher level. Hold your heels together, arms hanging at your side; stand erect, chin in, shoulders down, chest full, inhale and exhale easily; advance, stepping on the balls of your feet, moving your body forwardly with the advanced foot, alternately, without swaying your body to and fro.

Take a standing position four to eight feet from the person, with your right foot eight inches in advance and the weight of your body on the ball of your advanced foot; breathe and hold your chest full; stand before your man in a firm, still, serene manner; talk in a low, exalted, distinct tone of voice, without pauses, stuttering, fear, demurral, ambiguity, temper or bewilderment, and do it in a manly, courteous manner. Make your interview, conversation, proposition, brief and to the point.

When through, express your appreciation, make a graceful turn and walk away in the same manner and attitude as you approached. An exalted man always acts the nobleman. A gentleman may or may not be a nobleman. A gentleman is supposed to be well bred, but is usually a man of independent income, perhaps a titled man or entitled to bear a coat-of-arms. Practice this exercise and you can interview lords; accost chiefs; influence people of rank; meet mobs; address audiences; speak in the parliament; deliver a formal oration from the platform or an allocution to troops; a discourse from the pulpit; a scientific lecture before men of research; present a proposition to moneyed magnates; converse colloquially with people at large; promote business or public movements; and always *win,* because you have perfect control of every faculty, every act, every expression, every move of eyes, fingers and senses.

CULTIVATION OF FRIENDLINESS, JOY AND CHEERFULNESS—EXERCISE 9

Assume an exalted attitude; feel happy, thrill with joy; make yourself feel that all people are your friends, that you are their friend, that luck clings to you, that everything favors you. Take this exercise for ninety days, one-half hour each day.

DEVELOPMENT OF SELF COMPOSURE
AND NERVE CONTROL—EXERCISE 10

Sit like a statue of stillness, not supporting your back against the chair. Feel that there is something super eminent in you; that you have found yourself; that infinity lives within you; that your aspirations and attainments are sublime; that you are masterful and imposing; that your soul is serene; that your greatness is in yourself and not in superficial props; that your hearing is stately; mind lofty; address kingly or queenly; that you can act and cause other people to act; that you can make every move count; that nothing disturbs you; that you are sacred and self content; that you live in a high altitude of soul; that you are exclusive; that you have perfect control of tongue, fingers, functions and senses. Repeat all so that you can hear yourself say it and know that you believe it. Keep this up for twenty minutes.

Now center your mind on your own breath as it moves up and down in your chest, dwelling on your lofty qualities, and breathing thus for twenty minutes. Now elevate your arms slowly, holding your fingers limp and hanging down; keep elevating your arms until they are ten inches above your head, fingers still limp; now inhale a long breath and hold it, fingers still limp. Now begin to exert force in the uplifted arms, in the shoulders, neck, spine and chest, fingers still limp. Now send a will impulse or a blood current to the posterior crown of your head, until you feel a distinct movement of "something" in your brain substance. Then exhale and repeat, else retire and let nature complete the cell building that you have so efficiently started. You will be conscious of perfect nerve control, self composure, self mastery when you are through with this exercise. You will say: I never felt like this before.

You can take this exercise by itself for ninety days, always at the same hour, but read this course one hundred times before you begin with exercises or you cannot focus and dwell with your mind on exercises, states of mind, or of many different mental processes at the same time.

The foregoing exercises are neurostatic. You can change from one exercise to another alternately, take them according to your own plan or you can take one for ninety days in one stretch. You are practicing many different mental processes by taking these exercises, and by reading this course.

In the next lesson, Lesson 13, exercises particularly designed for phlegmatic people are presented. Read them whether you are phlegmatic or not, so you will understand the inherent principles behind the "balancing" of particular dispositions or temperaments.

MY FAVORITE POEM

I asked God for strength
   that I might achieve;
I was made weak
   that I might learn humbly to obey.
I asked for health
   that I might do greater things;
I was given infirmity
   that I might do better things.
I asked for riches
   that I might be happy;
I was given poverty
   that I might be wise.
I asked for power
   that I might have the praise of men;
I was given weakness
   that I might feel the need of God.
I asked for all things
   that I might enjoy life;
I was given life
   that I might enjoy all things.
I got nothing I asked for
   but everything I hoped for;
In spite of myself,
   my unspoken prayers were answered--
I am among all men
   mostly blessed.

-AUTHOR UNKNOWN

LESSON 13

NEURO-DYNAMIC EXERCISES
(TO AROUSE YOUR FORCES)

These exercises favor phlegmatic people. But, as there are not very many such people who take a course like this, we shall only mention one or two such exercises. At an occasional time, you may feel dull or weak headed, and one or two of such neuro-dynamic exercises may arouse you to life and action.

TENSION EXERCISES FOR NERVES
AND MUSCLES—EXERCISE 1

Stand and assume a strong attitude; inhale and exhale in a steady cumulative manner, so that each successive inhalation is longer than the preceding one, keeping this up for five breaths or more, without practicing forceful breathing. Then, take a few easy breaths; dwell upon your own exalted qualities; now inhale slowly and gradually as you elevate your arms slowly high above your head, clinching your fists and tensing arms, shoulders, neck, head, chest, stomach and lower limbs easily, slowly, gradually, as you inhale more and more air, without exhaling or releasing your tension, until you feel that you have exerted all your strength and that exhalation is imperative; now, with an effort of the will, slow down the tension just as gradually as you increased it.

Then take a few easy breaths and repeat the exercise once more or more than once. Use less force at first, but increase from month to month as your nerves, muscles and tissues grow stronger. This exercise calls most of your motor structures and motor nerves into action. It is a *dynamic* exercise.

FOR THE LOWER BODY AND
THE VENOUS CIRCULATION—EXERCISE 2

Assume a strong attitude dwelling upon the *Great Within*; inhale slowly as you raise your arms as high as you can, rising on your toes, inhaling air all the time, and bending your knees descend as low as you can, all of the time tensing slowly and increasingly. Now, rise up, exhale, decrease the tension slowly until you are completely relaxed; then take a few full breaths and repeat two or more times, being sure that you do not injure yourself by overuse of your motor equipment.

FOR MOST OF YOUR JOINTS—EXERCISE 3

Step forward; elevate your arms; spread your fingers; inhale and tense slowly and increasingly; bend your knees forwardly and downward, holding the air as you descend. Then exhale slowly and let go of the force by degrees so as to come to the original attitude. Breathe easily and repeat the exercise once or twice. This exercise may be taken four, eight, up to sixteen times, later on as you go on with the course but not at first.

FOR THE BONES—EXERCISE 4

To reach the bones, *will effort* must be used *persistently*. Shoulder some heavy weight, such as a plank, a small tree, a salt sack or a light weight man. Carry this weight for a long distance until you feel disinclined to carry it any longer. Now inhale air, and by effort of the will, carry the burden some distance longer. Then throw off the weight, inhale long, steady breaths and say in a strong voice: A man's will is a mighty power.

THE SECRET OF VIGOR, LIFE AND BEAUTY

Men of vigor, women of beauty, snatch the breath with ease and force. Their voice is distinct, face bright, step elastic, as oxygen steams them up. In fever, lung disease, flu and low states of vitality, respiration is short, shallow and faint. In youth, in health, inhalation is deep, rapid, prolonged and exhalation is slow. Air should enter lungs rather quickly, also with force; and leave the lungs rather slowly, to invite life and vigor.

If a dying man could take long, deep breaths with slow exhalations, he would probably not go beyond for many years. Instead, he uses the panting method of breathing, which, of course, is death breathing. Take short breaths and crop the breath quickly and you will soon become the surgeon's carving stuff. To cure diseases with pills, dope, vaccines and technique is an idle dream.

Correct breathing, self culture and a corrective diet are the keys to life, health, beauty, influence and accomplishment. Quick, deep inhalations vitalize when the air leaves the lungs silently. The most noticeable habit of a nobleman is his deep, quick, full inhalations and slow, silent exhalations. Other points of distinction are his full, large chest, lofty bearing, courteous manners, erect position, expanding nostrils, etc.

Look at the ample nostrils of the spirited orator as he pours out his pathos. Notice the heaving bosom of the loving maiden, her springy steps, beauty of complexion, glowing eyes, lively manners. Notice the chest movements of the happy lover. Compare the face, manners, walk, cheeks, eyes and chest movements, also the disposition of the pessimist, cynic, dyspeptic with those of the spirited orator, happy lover, enraptured maiden and learn a deep lesson in chest culture, animation, oxidation.

OXIDATION OR CHEST CULTURE AROUSING LAZY AIR CELLS IN YOUR LUNGS—EXERCISE 1

Stand erect on the balls of your feet; inhale and fill your lungs with air; rise on your toes and raise your arms as high as you can, inhaling more and more air, until your lungs are recharged. As you do this, fill your soul with exalted sentiments; now empty your lungs as completely as possible; repeat this exercise four times.

Double and treble the number of exercises in a few months, and it will arouse millions of lazy air cells in your lungs, promote oxidation, develop your chest, recharge your blood with fresh oxygen. Breathing should be a pleasure. Your lungs should drink in the air with the greatest eagerness, and your blood should absorb the oxygen also with great eagerness. Eating should be a pleasure, to be corrective and life building.

BREATHING THAT CALMS THE NERVES AND THE MIND—EXERCISE 2

Sit uprightly without chair back for support; breathe naturally inhaling rather deeply, quickly, forcefully and exhale slowly, silently so that you train your lungs to life-building habits of breathing. Keep this up for five minutes and empty your lungs completely; now lower your shoulders and let your arms hang lifeless at your sides, holding your chest out, chin in, still filling your mind with high thoughts of yourself; now center your mind upon the upward and downward movements of your own breath and keep this up for another five minutes, measuring the time without watching the clock or without mind concern; now, as you take a fresh breath slowly, raise your arms, spread your fingers, stretch and by the power of your will, send a will impulse to your crown where your sentiment of self exaltation has its seat. Repeat this last act six to ten times so as to intromit will impulse to the posterior crown of your head and thus animate and re-animate that special soul sensorium. This attracts fresh blood to the brain and stimulates cell building; it also arouses sleeping brain cells into action.

This exercise infuses a restful peace and makes you feel as serene as a placid lake. Take this exercise when you feel nervous or excited and you will be surprised at the favorable results.

Lesson 14 is next, and it completes our work with the mind by teaching ways to concentrate, again with the object of building self exaltation.

LESSON 14

HOW TO FOCUS THE MIND

Many people posses genius, but if they are scatterbrained, they cannot properly use their genius. There must be unity of mind, thought and effort. The word synergy means co-activity of mind and function. The man who can dwell on a wish, desire, problem, sentiment, thought, invention, study, transaction, etc., in a coherent, successive, connective and constructive manner for a long time, always wins, succeeds, learns his lessons, passes his examinations with high honors.

The power to unify the faculties, focus the eyes, continue in a successive manner with the same thought, sentiment or work; to bring together, weave, interweave, and consolidate thoughts and effort; to hold the mind attentively to one and the same operation; to involve and mobilize all the forces; to use and apply all the knowledge possessed; to eternalize mental processes in one and the same direction—that same power of the mind we call synergy, while some call it power of mental concentration.

But concentration is not the proper word to use in relation to those mental processes. Some people can concentrate, but they concentrate themselves into abstraction or absence of mind, until the mind becomes a blank. Again other people concentrate the mind so strongly that they cannot remove the mind from an invention, a grudge, a love emotion, and thus concentrate themselves into the asylum for the insane. Still other people can concentrate the mind for a few years on one and the same work, then change and concentrate just as strongly on some other occupation. In the course of a lifetime, one and the same man has been a salesman, a preacher, a politician, a lawyer, a railroad man, a gentleman farmer; in short, he has dabbled in fourteen different occupations always concentrating will, might and mind on the work in hand.

Does such a man lack power of mental concentration? Indeed not! He has a wonderful power of concentration. He can concentrate on any subject, thought, work, sentiment, invention; can reason and think like a Philadelphia lawyer; can learn and study anything and can even concentrate himself into the asylum. Men who can concentrate so strongly that they cannot stop their own thoughts, nor remove their minds from the question in hand, surely have wonderful powers of mental concentration. It is not concentration they lack so much as they lack power of self mastery, self regulation or the ability to act or not act in *unity* with certain faculties or with all of the faculties.

When the mind can act in unity so that there is harmony, co-activity, focalization, consolidation of thought, success of mind action, continuity without cessation in mental operations and can complete work or mental processes and also have power to slow up, to discontinue work, studies or mental processes at will—then, and not until then, do they have their mind under control. Some faculties enable us to concentrate; other faculties qualify us for self engineering; still other faculties focalize, unify, eternalize work or mental processes; while still other faculties enable us to *stop, restrain, relax, cease* mental processes, thoughts, plans, purposes, work, inventions, studies, desires, love, emotions, and so on.

Whatever this mental power should be called, we cannot consistently call it concentration. Mind mastery would be a better name. However, that mental power has not yet been named. Whatever it may be called, it should be developed. Mind mastery includes concentration, other mind processes, also the power to restrain, relax, cease mental activity without concentrating ourselves into the asylum.

MIND—EXERCISE 1

Focus your eyes and mind on a moving bird, train or automobile so strongly that you do not see, hear or cognize its forward flight. Rivet your eyes and mind on that one object, though you see it no longer, but keep the picture persistently in your mind and before your eyes for one to three minutes, using your mind and eyes like a lens in a camera. You will probably take this exercise one hundred to three hundred times before you succeed because your eyes and mind have never been trained to processes of focalization. It is an important exercise, but difficult to master for some time.

MENTAL CO-ACTIVITY PRACTICE
AND MIND CESSATION BY WILL—EXERCISE 2

Think of a subject persistently and give all your faculties an opportunity to act; bide your time and see what other thoughts or facts you can bring to bear upon that subject from every angle. Think how it would affect your friends, parents, children, laws, country, religion, science, philosophy, art, music, dress, industry, health, life, disease, business, wages, humanity, politics and everything you can think of, for twenty minutes to a half hour, so you may give most of your faculties an opportunity to act upon the subject. Then, suddenly release your mind deliberately so there is a complete cessation.

Develop mind mastery so you can master concentration, attention, meditation at will and you will not concentrate yourself into abstraction nor into the asylum. It is not enough that we are able to concentrate, we should also be able to stop the mind in order to be masters over mind, thought and mental concentration. We must learn to stop thought, cease concentration, discontinue dwelling on desires, insults, wrongs, wrath, inventions or whatever else may occupy the mind, so we may have full mastery of the mind at all times and under all circumstances.

After you have read this course about one hundred times and incorporated it into mind, heart and soul; after you have taken the various exercises over and over again and you can focus your mind, bring all of your faculties to synthetic co-activity, concentration, etc., you will be able, by will effort, to recess or mind cessation—you will have reached that desirable power of *mind mastery* which leads to self exaltation.

"I sought my God and could not find Thee. I searched for my soul but it eluded me. Then I looked for my brother and found all three."

Two "kids" of the eighties. Photo by Leslie.

FINAL THOUGHTS

It is very clear to me, in dealing with sick people, that we have to separate ourselves from sickness in order to be well.

There is a difference in what I call kingdoms. Kingdoms, to me, are the *Kings'* domains. We live on different levels of consciousness and in different kingdoms.

I want to bring this out because it has meant so much to me. I am so glad that I saw this. It didn't come like thunder out of the heavens but came very slowly. However, I sometimes wondered why things didn't go faster. We are constantly on trial, so overcome with disturbances that we often impede our own development. We are unable to see the beauty before us. We converse but cannot comprehend. We have been blinded by our inattention to the matters within us. All enlightenment comes from within.

Eyes alone can see eight million vibrations of colors. Just imagine the many different levels of vibration. There are only seven primary colors but when divided into individual wave frequencies, they multiply into millions of colors.

A tree itself stands in spectacular existence with no regard to its life form. In its very being, it expounds strength and longevity. Mere existence depends upon nature, environment and the elements bestowed upon it. There is no decision made to develop from within outwardly, it simply is.

Man, on the other hand, has choices. Choices to make changes and live in an environment he chooses, on the level he chooses. He can make a difference.

His choice to reach for the *divine* teachings on the spiritual level allows a strength beyond explanation.

Once you have traveled on this level of consciousness, you will find absolute harmony. There is peace, a healthy within, that is unshakable. You will have something that no one can disturb.

We cannot live just for our thoughts. We cannot live just for the mind. There are many states and senses we must combine to create the whole oneness with ourselves and the world. I feel grateful and thankful that I have an opportunity to *feel* in this other world.

You become "*light* hearted." It is not until you see the light will you be uplifted. Christ said, "I am the light of the world." He is the one that adds color to your life and He offers a new dimension entirely. As I said before, many people hear of the Christ, not realizing that He is talking about another kingdom. I will show you a better way of life. I will open a door for you and all you have to do is reach for it. You must desire it.

Then I awaken and say, "Oh, what a foolish person I am to want the glorious things in life, when it is already written, "All that I have is thine."

My days in Tibet. Photo by Marie.

WHAT WE ARE DEEPEST, WE REALLY ARE

There is a desperate need to go beyond the stage of today's environment, both inner and outer. Hating is killing. So is living in smog-congested cities, wearing glasses that filter out ultraviolet rays from the sun, living behind glass windows and working all day in frozen, dark and dreary workrooms. All these are destructive to the physical, mental and spiritual well-being of mankind.

Light and many other forms of vibration are needed to awaken the life force of mankind. A successful day is one of joy. Radiant and beautiful colors bring joy. Beautiful flowers will balance our mental attitude to live a more balanced day.

In the living garden, we know that red is quickening; yellow is for happiness and good cheer; orange gives us assurance and assistance in our nervous expression; blue is for the cooling off periods; green for repair and rebuilding the cell structure; indigo answers our higher callings.

We should all go to the rainbow, for it is all around us. It has been written that God has made a covenant with man, other living creatures and the Earth to bring life through His rainbow. These streaming, vibrant colors are our lifeline, our cord to the Divine.

Sociologists today claim that man is a product of his outer environment. They forget man truly lives from within.

The foods for our body are made up of elements potentized by the sun, by light and by color.

We find that when a plant is placed in darkness, it will even deform itself in its attempt to reach the light. We, too, share this direct relationship between light and our life pattern.

We need to be closer to Nature and be nearer to ideas and thoughts *for* one another. Good should be our goal. We must learn how to make all humans a success, but it seems we live in museum of mistakes.

How can be change this? We can start by realizing that people are more important than things and the inner self is more important than the outer.

Education, training and learning may be dangerous unless we consider that whatever we do is done for all of mankind's eternal good. What is the use of working to heal the physical body...to cleanse, purify and eliminate without cleansing the *mind* of old debris, negative thinking and actions?

My friend and former patient, Dr. Elisabeth Caspari, an educator in the Montessori tradition, has said, "The soul needs to be nourished as much as the...body...it is a way of life. The unique personality of each soul must be assisted in its unfoldment. All of the finer qualities of the spirit are inherent as a divine heritage within the child." We cannot nourish the soul or develop our gifts by negative thinking.

The psychologists say we only use 10% of our mental faculties. It is hard to believe that 90% of our brain lies dormant. One of the universities, when checking an average man's thinking for a 24-hour day, found that 60% of his thinking was negative, harmful and deleterious to his nervous system, heart activity and tissue repair.

This means that nearly two-thirds of our daily thinking, which is only 10% of our capacity, is of an ailing, destructive nature.

We certainly do need an expansion of consciousness, a moving into awareness to use all of our being.

Skylab is already using color in infrared, ultraviolet photographs and is working to view the planet Earth in 13 different wavelengths. Why shouldn't physicians who recognize physical manifestations and physical achievements work in other vibrations as well? Why not see the possibilities of mind expansion?

Color is the universal language of understanding. It is cleansing, peaceful and harmonious to everyone. You can bring the soul to life through the use of certain colors.

A red-hot temper needs the cooling influence of blue. Without violet-indigo in our spectrum, we have knowledge without love. We need all of the chemical elements to be balanced in our body, and we need all corresponding tints of colors for spiritual balance.

BEYOND THE PHYSICAL REALM

Man is a physical being, but we have the opportunity to be metaphysical. I am a firm believer that the body and the mind should be the servants to the spirit. Communication between men could be more successful through color, with its spiritual and mental counterparts. We find that there are aesthetic sensations produced by color that cause reactions upon the human body. It is the direct application of color through the body that harmonizes assimilation, revitalization, endurance and stamina. We have to replace color energies in our bodies as they are dissipated.

What we are deepest is what we really are. This is where uplifting, good feelings and inspiration exist. Existing in the physical and external comforts is only a small part of the whole man and a very poor one. Contentment comes from within. This inner contentment "colors" our existence and produces a more abundant life for this material world.

Today we are working on the expansion of the mind to recognize beauty. It is not easy for a man to say, "Look for more beauty in your life if you are to be well inwardly."

Let the interior decorations of your home be light and cheerful. This will benefit your family, friends and your own development. A human soul cannot unfold in dark rooms and stuffy air. The heart cannot function normally in murky dwellings. Love does not thrive in a dull atmosphere. Let your soul broaden out. There is romance in stillness, love in cheerful interior decorations and joy in a healthy home.

It isn't only Edward Bach who saw the healing properties of the flower. We can all share in these wonders.

John Ott found that the greatest influence on the body by color is done through the retina. Millions of rods and cones are there to bring the message to the brain. This is demonstrated by an experiment with a chameleon. As you may know, this animal changes colors according to his environment. When one eye is covered, only half of his body changes color accordingly.

The range of known vibration is tremendous, extending from cosmic rays and gamma rays through X-rays, ultraviolet, visible light, infrared rays, heat, wireless and radio waves.

BEYOND THE VISUAL SPECTRUM

Vibrational energies above and below the visual spectrum are extremely powerful. Long-wave vibrations, such as some types of sound waves, can pass through buildings. Heat vibrations can cook our food but also kill many types of living things such as enzymes and germ life. Scientists say every physical object is susceptible to a certain vibration that will cause it to break or explode.

Short-wave vibrations, such as gamma rays, cosmic rays and X-rays, are only partly understood, but the most powerful forms of radiation can penetrate deep into the earth.

A space age micro-device that fits on the head of a pin may be able to analyze much about a patient from a single drop of blood. The device, using ion-specific field effect transducers, works by measuring electrically-charged ions in living tissue.

Radiation, properly used, can kill cancer cells; improperly used, it can destroy healthy tissue. X-ray fluoroscopes, commonly used in shoe stores many years ago to determine the fit of shoes, were discontinued when found to be causing cancer. Overexposure to X-ray radiation is extremely dangerous, and both poorly designed color TV sets and improperly filtered X-ray scanners in medical and dental clinics have exposed millions of persons to dangerous and unnecessary radiation.

John Villforth, director of the National Center for Biologics and Radiological Health, claims that as much as 30% of diagnostic X-rays are unnecessary.

Nuclear bombs produce deadly radiation which destroy life by passing through the body and killing cells through ionization. Symptoms of toxic radiation exposure range from lack of appetite, headache, nausea, vomiting and diarrhea to sterility, blood diseases, cataracts, cancer and leukemia.

Back at the other end of the vibrational scale, much safer than X-rays, is heat-sensor technology. Cameras have been developed which can take photographs of temperature variations of the body, a low-frequency technology which doesn't put radiation into us. Such photos can be used to spot nerve damage, muscle spasm sites, circulatory blocks, stress spots and developing breast tumors. It can spot the latter sooner than

X-rays, according to experts. Fractures, previous surgery, cuts and any old injuries that have produced physical changes in the body are shown. The latest machine to take these pictures uses liquid crystals. Although the thermogram, as it is called, must be used with other forms of diagnosis and analysis, it is considered one of the more promising tools of space-age health. An infection will show up as a reddish or yellowish area. The "coolest" areas start with chocolate brown and change as body areas grow warmer to tan, salmon, yellow, green and dark blue. Dark blue represents the hottest places. The thermogram is considered so reliable that it is used as court evidence in whiplash cases, to prove or disprove a person's claim to back injury undetectable by X-rays.

Another space-age system for examinations has been developed by General Electric scientists. This new system doesn't use chemicals or radiation, but magnetism and sound rays. The machine uses a 9-ton magnet 20,000 times more powerful than the Earth's magnetic field, allowing analysis of body and brain areas that previously could be checked only by exploratory surgery. Called the NMR system (nuclear magnetic resonance), it can see through bones and into cells, providing an image and a chemical analysis.

EVERYTHING HAS ITS OWN VIBRATION

Every healthy tissue and every pathological form of tissue has its particular rating of vibration. These are observed and can or will be measured correctly by photography, thermogram, percussion, nuclear magnetic resonance (NMR), ultrasound or other method, by delicately attuned instruments accurately recording the vibratory rate of the congested tissue. Using electromagnetic waves for a reading, the vibratory energy of the discordant rate associated with disease can be revealed. Scientists are perfecting instruments for this work, and it is estimated that 9 out of 10 cancers can be detected by the various new methods.

Just as thermography and the NMR system provide extremely sensitive diagnosis, the aura of the inner man will be the key to diagnosis in the future. Seeing inside the body in the safest possible way is the desire of the entire healing art.

The ultimate step is when the patient realizes that only by changing the inner self can deficiencies be filled in with light and beauty resulting in total physical rejuvenation. As we work in harmony through the *Great Within*, we awaken our love nature and develop compassion. Our diets and thoughts change from a deeper level, and all of these positive energies are evident in the aura.

On the material level, it is not by chance that we should have beautiful color in the foods we eat. It is not a random process that makes a grape purple or red, that makes a pear yellow, that gives an apple a crimson hue. When feeding upon this food, you should visually enjoy these colors, for the eyes assimilate color as the digestive system assimilates nutrients. *It helps you to be beautiful to partake of beauty.* As we take in these blessed things we see, feel and taste, remember that there are also mental things chosen with the same idea; selected and added to our vibratory rate. We use it for radiation of these fine mineral elements within the body.

I am sure that Luther Burbank talked to his flowers. He said he never hired anyone who did not have a love for plant life. So, I believe his mental vibrations were conveyed to the plants, for they did respond. This "green thumb" is evident when we have the magnetic power of healing in our aura. This is why such a wonderful garden developed under Burbank's fingers.

It was Michelet who said, "Of all flowers, it is the human flower who has the greatest need of the sun." It was the Greeks who were the most "modern" of ancient people using sunlight for baths and worshipping their sun god, Apollo. But, modern research has shed much more light on ways in which our bodies need sunlight, especially ultraviolet.

Scientists received 53,000 pictures from one space satellite in less than three months. This multispectral scanner detected various polluted and disease-ridden areas of the Earth. Why shouldn't we explore the space between our ears for pollution and impurities?

Radiate that which will grow and expand to every corner of your being, and this flowering of the mind will express beauty and attract the finer side of life.

The future healing of the human being will begin when we radiate this colorful life. The well-being of our cell structure depends on what it receives from our thinking and feeling. While we are building this temple of beauty within, let us remember that we know each other by the countenance we express. Our living is conveyed in levels of color.

In the present, we live for what we have and can get. In the future, we must live for what we can give and pour forth. This is the healing way. We try to vibrate with our possessions from outside the body, but the future will recognize we are richest when we give forth radiantly from within.

WE ARE VIBRANT BEINGS

It is awesome to realize that the origin of life is in vibration. The great scientist, Albert Einstein, proved that matter and energy are equivalent, and we find that an accumulation of vibrations provides the substance and form to energy that gives rise to matter. All matter is vibration.

In the beginning, the most delicate vibrations probably came into existence as color. It has been suggested that light is the basis of form and activity in matter. Studies have demonstrated that light of different colors affects germ life, insects, plants, animals and people in different ways. There is something inside us that recognizes and responds to different colors.

Colors have found their way into a number of common expressions in many different languages. In the United States, we have many such references. People say, "He's looking at the world through rose-colored glasses," meaning that a person is happy and optimistic, sometimes unrealistically so. We refer to "blue Monday," implying a depressive state. We hear, "He saw red," meaning that the man became very angry. "He has a yellow streak down his back," means that person is considered a coward. When a new employee is referred to as "green," it means he or she is inexperienced. "You're in the pink," is a slang expression indicating good health. We occasionally hear someone speak of a "black night of despair," which, interestingly enough, relates one of the worst mental conditions to the absence of light.

Research continues to uncover uses for specific colors of light. Certain pure colors, projected on a screen where hospital patients viewed them, were found to accelerate healing. Painting the walls of prisons and mental institutions certain shades reduces the tendency to violence. A certain type of liver malfunction in newborn infants can be corrected by blue light.

The Russians are using laser light on acupuncture points to correct some conditions. Sunlight on the skin converts a type of cholesterol into vitamin D.

Every living thing has its own vibration and responds to other vibrations. There are vibrations in minerals and gems so fine that we can't even detect them with the senses. The finer vibrations may have more healing power than we would suspect. If we understood more about the finer vibrations and their sources, perhaps we could find better ways of achieving the health level we seek.

To raise the health level, it is necessary for us to attract vibrations to replace those lost when body tissues and cells wear out from physical or mental overwork. We could recuperate and rebuild, revitalize and rejuvenate our bodies if we knew how to find and use the finer forces. I believe that the electromagnetic field that surrounds and inter-penetrates the human body is altered by the foods we eat, the thoughts and emotions we express, so that certain vibrations are attracted and repelled from us. We may draw violence or peace to ourselves. We may draw health or dis-ease. There are people so disassociated from the natural state of their bodies that they are "out of this world," so to speak. They bring harm to themselves and to the society they live in.

We live in this vibratory world, and it is time we begin to learn how to reach for the vibrations that help us make the best of our lives.

To achieve optimum health and well-being, there are four areas of study we need to take up: vibration, music, color, and God and Nature. If we did this, we would find an energy to heal us and lift us up. We would find our path in life. We would know what sort of climate, altitude and environment to live in to feel best and to do our best. We would know what clothing to wear, what friends to associate with, what to talk about to attract and sustain well-being. Our marriages, jobs and lives would change.

There is reportedly a very highly-paid consultant who designs color patterns for factories to reduce on-the-job accidents. Is it an accident that more speeding tickets are given to drivers of red automobiles? Is the term "red light district" a whimsical choice of words? Colors have a tremendous impact on our lives.

In India, for many centuries, teachers of yoga have described seven basic chakras, or energy centers in the body which correspond to the colors of the rainbow. Scripture says, "I do set my (rain)bow in the cloud, and it shall be for a token of a covenant between me and the earth." Some researchers claim that the energy flares and coronas revealed in Kirlian photography are related to the electromagnetic field that flows through our acupuncture points. Others agree and add that this is the aura spoken of since ancient times, the spiritual "rainbow" worn personally by each human being. In a sense, the rainbow is a symbol of the life that God sustains on the Earth, not simply material life, but life in its mental and spiritual sense, including life rich in vibrational qualities. Life is health but more than health. Life is work but more than work. Life is marriage but more than marriage. The vibrations that constantly go forth from our bodies and are received by them play a tremendous part in our lives.

THE ART OF USING COLOR

Expansion of consciousness to serve mankind could best be done through the awareness of the values of color. For years, I have been experimenting with the development of beauty through colors. Beauty is one of our most neglected mind factors in daily life.

It would be a time of healing to open our consciousness and dwell for awhile in the beauties of nature through color. I do this for my patients by encouraging them to blend colors in several media—finger painting, flower gardening, clothing, redecorating homes and taking walks in the country.

I also suggest putting up beautiful color photographs around the house. Photographs demonstrate color in a lovely form. In this color therapy work, I take many pictures of nature showing unusual visions of the usual. One photo may indicate the delicate shades and hues of several types of flowers, another may focus on the inside of a single flower, and still another may give testimony to the contrast of the colors of nature.

In times of isolation, it is nature and color that may bring us back into reunion with the universe. By absorbing these colors daily, you will find you are feeding your body and your soul. Use these pictures in your everyday life. Set them on your dresser, living room table, work desk and kitchen counter. This is to develop your awareness of beauty which may need activating from the subconscious. Our sense of beauty, color and harmony already lives deep within us and may only need to be awakened.

Expressing this language of color is something everyone wants to do, for this is a *world* of color. We are all artists and project these feelings from our subconscious mind to change our awareness.

We need to bring this beauty to consciousness.

Everyone can appreciate a beautiful flower, a friendly dog, a glowing sunset or a radiant man or woman. When we open up our consciousness and dwell in the beauties of nature, we allow healing to enter our lives. The presence of God within extracts the values that we need from each "colorful" experience.

When we are present in beauty, we are absent from our sickness, our negative feelings. This is "out-picturing" the darkness of gloom from our lives, and should be our goal.

When God made the promise that all living things should have life through the rainbow, he certainly meant human beings as well as plant and animal life. If certain colors can help to change the sex life of animals, double the growth of certain plants, shrivel the pituitary glands of rats; make natural laxatives in yellow seeds, flowers and vegetation; create liver cleansers in the red beet, astringents in blackberries, greens for purification and supplying trace minerals; then there is cause for the doctor to investigate the benefits that may be derived from the influence and radiations of colors.

Goethe, on his dying bed, said, "Give man more light."

Life Interpreted Through Color

"O ye who seek to solve the knot,
Ye live in God and know him not.
Ye sit upon the river's brink,
Yet crave in vain a drop to drink;
Ye dwell beside a boundless store,
Yet perish, hungry, at the door."
"O, sometime comes to soul and sense
The Feeling which is evidence,
That very near about us lies,
The realm of spirit mysteries."

—John Greenleaf Whittier

The pattern of life to be
We weave in colors all our own.
And in the field of destiny
We reap as we have sown.

—John Greenleaf Whittier

Spring blew trumpets of color,
* Her green ran in my brain;*
I saw a blind man groping
* Tap, tap with his cane.*
I pitied him in his blindness
* But, can I boast I see?*
Perhaps there walks a spirit
* Close by who pities me.*

A spirit who sees me tapping
* The fine sense cane of my mind*
Amid such unseen glories—
* I may be worse than blind.*

113

Like colors in a rainbow
The human prism lives:
From red to violet
He radiates—
And all the while he is just what he gives.

The Touch of the Master's Hand

'Twas battered and scarred, and the auctioneer
Thought it scarcely worth his while
To waste much time on the old violin.
But he held it up with a smile.
"What am I bidden good folk?" he cried.
"Who'll start the bidding for me?
A dollar—a dollar—then two, only two—
Two dollars, and who'll make it three
Going for three"—but no—
From the room far back, a gray-haired man
Came forward and picked up the bow,
Then, wiping the dust from the old violin,
And tightening the loosened strings,
He played a melody pure and sweet
As a caroling angel sings.
The music ceased and the auctioneer,
With a voice that was quiet and low,
Said, "NOW what am I bid for the old violin?"
And he held it up with the bow.
"A thousand and who'll make it two"
Two thousand and who'll make it three?
Three thousand once—three thousand twice—
And going—and gone, cried he.
The people cheered, but some of them cried,
We do not understand.
What changes its worth? Quickly came the reply,
"The touch of the Master's hand."
And many a man with life out of tune,
And battered and scarred with sin,
Is auctioned cheap to a thoughtless crowd,
Much like the old violin.

114

A mess of pottage—a glass of wine,
    A game—and he travels on;
He is going once—and going twice—
    He's going—and almost gone.
But the master comes, and the foolish crowd
    Never can quite understand
The worth of a soul, and the change that's wrought
    By the Touch of the Master's Hand

If You've Enjoyed Reading This Book . . .

Vibrant Health From Your Kitchen—One of Dr. Jensen's latest and greatest books. In this book, he teaches the basics of health and nutrition. A food guide for family health and well-being. The reader learns how proper foods can overcome certain mineral deficiencies, allergies and build immunity.

Food Healing of Man—Innumerable experiences are recounted in Dr. Jensen's work with both human beings and animals. The book is a comprehensive layman's guide to the healing power of foods elaborating on nutritional deficiencies. Lists 28 factors necessary for correcting body ailments. A study is made as to why foods heal and the reason for supplements.

Nature Has A Remedy—Solutions applying nature's restorative powers are discussed. A nature encyclopedia covering hundreds of ailments. Teaches methods of taking care of various symptoms encountered with diet, water treatments, physical exercise, climate, environment and others.

Tissue Cleansing Through Bowel Management—Toxic-laden tissues can become a breeding ground for disease. Elimination organs, especially the bowel, must be properly taken care of. This book tells the reader how. Bowel management through a balanced nutritional program with adequate fiber in the diet and regular exercise can often do wonders. A special 7-day cleanse will bring back energy, regenerate tissues and allow good food to let nature do its healing work.

The Healing Mind Of Man—The spiritual, mental and physical qualities of man must be considered for healing. All body functions depend upon our mind, and must be brought into balance before healing can occur.

A New Lifestyle For Health and Happiness—A concise summary of Dr. Jensen's most effective methods for restoring and maintaining good health. A sound program outlined with practical applications and daily charts for improving a person's lifestyle.

Vital Foods For Total Health, A Cook Book And Kitchen Guide—You are what you eat! Your health, your looks, and even the length of your life is affected by your diet. Your meals may look good and taste good, yet lack the vital elements your body requires. So to keep your health and your looks, or to regain them, eat correctly! This book will tell you how. This is a complete cookbook which combines health teaching and the newer knowledge of nutrition.

Foods That Heal—In the first half of this book, Dr. Jensen focuses on the philosophy and ideas of Hippocrates, the brilliant work of Dr. V. G. Rocine, and concludes with a look at his own pioneering work in the field of nutrition. The second half is a nutritional guide to fruits and vegetables.

For information on *Dr. Jensen's Food Products for the 21st Century* and for a *free* catalog of all his books and supplies, please write to:

Dr. Bernard Jensen
24360 Old Wagon Road
Escondido, CA 92027